MOLOTOV COCKTAILS

Anna Mandoki

MOLOTOV COCKTAILS

Originally published in Australia in 2006 by Wild & Woolley, an imprint of Books & Writers Network Pty Ltd, PO Box W76, Watsons Bay NSW 2030

Design and cover photograph by Anna Mandoki

ISBN 978 1 74018 378 9

Some of the names in this book have been changed at the request of the persons concerned.

My story is very simple, I'm no hero. But many of us little people, small persons, make the whole thing.
—István Pálos

RED LETTER

THE PLANE from Melbourne lands in Vienna. There are four hours to kill before my connecting flight to Budapest.

I clear customs and scan the concourse, searching for a place to buy chocolate. After twenty-two hours cramped in economy, feeling bloated from airline food and lack of exercise, and with the journey not yet over, a sugar hit is exactly what I need. My body believes it is the middle of the afternoon, but in Vienna it is early – the shops won't be open for at least another hour. So I step through a double layer of sliding glass doors, and inhale the air outside the terminal.

It is six in the morning, on the lighter edge of dawn, and the shock of cold snatches my breath away. A pearly haze has settled close to the ground. The fog obscures a car park directly opposite, and shrouds tall grey buildings to my right. The noise of early morning traffic, not yet in full flow, comes softly through the mist. I watch the travelers with their bleached faces and bleary eyes as they drag heavy suitcases across the road towards me, their bodies swollen by layers of jumpers, padded jackets and scarves.

It looks like any other airport terminal – architecturally anonymous, bleak and grey. But it feels like Europe; it's a feeling I remember. The sharp air is intoxicating. Drawn here again by an old, red letter, I know I have arrived.

The letter sits on my desk back in Melbourne: six crisp sheets a little smaller than A4. The paper still sharply white even though it will soon be a decade old. The sheets are covered on one side with

3

words tapped out slowly on a typewriter, letter by painful letter. The words run right up to the edges of the paper and sometimes beyond – a letter 'a' lies sliced in half, the missing piece perhaps still visible somewhere on the typewriter's cylinder. A small part of the story that has been left behind.

And like the paper, the ink has held its colour: the words are a rich cherry red. The diacritical marks – beyond the scope of an English typewriter – have been added later by hand, like afterthoughts. They are small flecks of scarlet pen, hundreds of them, dancing above the vowels.

The date is at the top: 1996.10.31, written in the European way. October 31 is my mother's birthday. I wondered what she was doing while my father tapped out his red letter key by slow key, at the typewriter installed on the polished dining room table in Gloucester, England. Perhaps she was at her job with the Civil Service; or perhaps she had taken her early retirement package by then and was watching Countdown on television, trying out the word puzzles for herself on a pad of paper, a cup of milky coffee by her side. She would have been fifty-four years old that day.

'*Kedves Lányom*', the letter begins. Dear Daughter.

While my brother and I were growing up, my father never spoke Hungarian. He preferred to struggle with English in an effort to fit in, not realising he would always be considered an outsider. Later on, I tried to learn his language, but it was too late – the contorted grammar has stayed foreign to me, frustratingly out of reach.

One recent summer, I was returning books to my local library when I passed two young women on a tree-lined Melbourne street. They stood close together, loose-limbed from the heat, sheltering in the shade. Their melancholy sentences, downward sloping, were unmistakeable. I lingered, trying to catch a sliver of meaning. It was in vain. The cadences flew straight to my heart, but the words locked me out.

At other times, I have heard English spoken with my father's heavy accent. Every syllable weighted equally, the rhythm of it dropping like slow, steady rain on a tin roof. I remember as a child feeling embarrassed when he spoke. I thought it was funny that he read the newspaper so laboriously, and couldn't write or spell. It made him seem dull and slow.

He never told me his story, not until much later, when I finally grew curious enough to ask. By then, I was living on the other side of the world. He took out his typewriter and wrote it all down for me, the story too long, the remembering too complex, for a conversation in English over the telephone.

The first time I tried to read his red letter, I felt like the dull one, struggling to understand. It took me longer to read, word by word and with the aid of a dictionary, than it must have taken him to type. The second reading, several years later when I was curious again, came more easily. This time, I was transported rapidly, magically, into a European winter. The words evoking another world, an extraordinary moment in history.

* * *

Hungary, close to the border with Austria, Boxing Day 1956

It is late in the evening, close to eleven o'clock. The deep silence of the countryside at night hangs over the fields. A thick layer of snow covers the ground.

Five young men are out in the open, on foot. They move slowly, without talking, in single file. My father, Péter Mándoki, leads the way in his bulky winter coat and heavy boots. He has chosen this field for its line of fruit trees. The men glide from the safety of one trunk to the next, keeping one man to a tree at all times. The angular branches are bare. The border is only five kilometres away, but the men are nervous and watchful. Their progress is slow.

5

Suddenly, my father catches the faint sound of voices directly ahead. Instinctively, he throws himself to the ground. The others see him drop and soon all five of them are lying flat on the crisp snow. Péter raises his head from the ground and strains to see in the darkness.

Roughly a hundred metres away, where he guesses the edge of the field must be, he makes out two men strolling through the snow. He thinks they are in uniform – soldiers. Péter listens, and waits.

The two men stop walking. There is a brief flash of flame, followed by the red glow of cigarettes. They stand and talk. Their voices carry well on the clear air. Péter struggles to make out the words, but isn't able to catch their meaning. He's certain now that they are Russian soldiers. Who else would stand so casually out in the fields, in the dark and the cold, close to the border like that?

Péter lies perfectly still. He keeps his breathing quiet and shallow, and the air in front of his lips barely stirs. The sharp bite of snow recedes before the heat of his fear. He tries to become part of the white earth, to blend seamlessly in with the bare, black trees, the silent and empty night. So that a glance in his direction will pass right over him, see nothing but landscape. As if he had always been there.

The land is a part of my father, its moods and seasons run in his blood. Born at the foot of the Zemplén ranges, near the Slovakian border, the forests were his playground, the fields and vineyards his workplace. The vegetables on his table were grown in the family's small yard – potatoes, carrots, tomatoes, cucumber and onions. They had cows to provide milk, the liquid warm and frothing in a tin bucket on cool mornings close to dawn. Chickens scraped around in the mud of the yard, and rabbits scrabbled at the floors of their wire cages. The shed beside the outhouse always held one or two dark-skinned, foul smelling pigs. Sitting on the toilet, Péter would hear them shuffling around close beside him, slamming against the wooden boards.

And there was always plenty of wine to drink, drawn from barrels in the family cellar. Nourished by the rich volcanic soil of the hills, the pale, sweet grapes were left to wither and rot on the vine before picking, just ahead of the first frosts of winter. The wine they produced was sweet and oily, a deep golden brown, with a powdery sediment that settled at the bottom of the glass. The sickly scent of it tainted the breath of the men in the house.

Even though my father is a long way from his village, he feels at home out in the open fields. The earthy smell of the tree trunk beside him feels familiar, so does the crisp touch of the snow. This is his land. He stays quietly where he is, and waits for the soldiers to move on.

After a while, his patience is rewarded. The uniformed men finish their cigarettes. They turn and head back the way they came.

When they are out of sight, Péter pushes himself upright. He signals to his friends that the way ahead is clear. Snow sticks to him in a thin layer. He manages to brush most of it off, but icy water has seeped into the fabric of his coat, making it hang heavily on him. His boots are sodden, and drag his feet down. Moving carefully but with greater urgency now, he reaches the edge of the field. Where the Russians had been standing a short time ago, there is a dirt road. Péter checks in both directions. There is no sign of the soldiers. He waits for the others to catch up.

On the far side of the narrow, muddy road there are no more fields. They have reached the edge of a dense wood, and the deeper blackness between the tightly packed trunks beckons them on. Among the frozen trees they all feel safer, less exposed. Relaxing a little, they make good time despite the thick layer of snow that still tugs at their boots. Their breathing comes hard from the exertion, leaving fog trails in the frosty air.

7

Péter takes comfort from the trees, the soil-scented darkness, snow crunching underfoot. In his village, he and his friends used to drive an oxcart into the forest every winter, gathering wood to sell in the nearby town of Tokaj. It was an illegal, but critical, source of extra income over the long, lean winter months. While the ox grazed, the young men ranged through the forest collecting wood. Chopping it into manageable pieces, they brought it back to the cart. It would take a whole day to get a full load.

By nightfall, they would be ready to hitch up the ox and make the long journey across country, steering clear of major roads to minimise the risk of being caught. Progress was slow, the cart's wooden wheels rattling and jumping over rough ground. It was always close to dawn by the time they reached Tokaj. There, on the bank of the Tisza, where the river bends before the stone bridge at the centre of town, Péter and his friends would set up for business. In the towns, wood was difficult to come by, and their load would be quickly sold. Then there was the trip back home, which took up the whole of the following day. Thirty-six hours straight without sleep.

So Péter is used to this kind of journey; but in unfamiliar territory, among the trees, he finds it hard to steer a straight path. There are four men in the group, and the responsibility of leadership starts to weigh heavily on him. Doubts cloud his mind. Could he have taken a wrong turn, and be leading them all into danger? He tries to estimate how far they have travelled, how long they have been walking. The border must still be ahead – surely he could not have unknowingly doubled back? But time passes without any change in the landscape, and his anxiety grows.

Then without warning they are upon it – a strip of land cleared of all vegetation. The open space is as wide and straight as a road, and stretches away in both directions as far as they can see. On the opposite side the trees begin again, as dense as before.

'The *nyomsáv!*'

They have all heard of it: the belt of cleared land that runs along the border, often treacherous with landmines, and regularly patrolled. Their spirits soar – Austria and freedom are within sight. All they can think of is crossing the strip immediately, reaching the other side. But Péter cautions them.

'A Russian patrol could be nearby. We can't afford to make a mistake now.'

Hanging back close to the trees, the five men listen for any slight sound: the faint drift of voices, the crunching of feet in snow, a snap of twigs caused by the brush of a uniformed body against a tree trunk. But the only interruption to the stillness comes from their own exhausted breathing. Finally, as convinced as they can be that there are no patrols around, they sprint together across the exposed space. As he runs, Péter expects all the time to hear the calm silence shattered by a shout or volley of gunfire. But no sound comes. Each of them safely reaches the other side.

From this point on, the terrain slopes steeply downwards. The air is icy and brittle, too cold for snow to fall. They have not gone far beyond the cleared strip when Péter notices something among the trees – something that doesn't belong. It's a narrow bench on the ground, roughly hewn out of wood. He makes his way over and examines it more closely. There is enough space for a single person to sit and rest.

'Do you see that?' he says to the others, pointing at the snow beneath the bench.

He stoops to inspect the ground, his breath misting in the bitter air. Suddenly and without warning, the rattle of machine gun fire tears the night apart.

THE DOOR opens unexpectedly, before I have a chance to knock. Both of the Fehérs are standing in the doorway to greet me. They must have been watching from the window as I strolled up their driveway. I wonder if their eagerness is because they can't wait to share their stories. Or because they are simply anxious, and want it to be over.

Mr Fehér takes my old leather jacket, handling it as if it were a precious thing. His hair is soft and white, but his eyebrows are darker and coarse – they lend a solemn gravity to his wide, apple-cheeked face. He has a vague and enigmatic smile. His wife is slight and brisk, her brown hair neat, practical. Her straight-cut fringe makes her seem younger than she probably is.

I have come to meet them because the six short pages of my father's letter, on my desk at home, are not enough for me. The Hungarian Uprising of 1956 was an extraordinary and momentous event, a turning point in the Cold War. To view that event through a single man's eyes would be to simplify it, and restrict it.

From historical accounts I have learnt a little more: how the instability following Stalin's death in 1953 turned the satellite states of Eastern Europe into a ticking time bomb. That Hungary was the place where it would explode. I have trawled through the black-and-white words of the history books, through their stark facts, stripped of emotion and of personal stories – the things that matter the most. They have only sparked my interest, and left me ravenous to know more.

It's this hunger then, a need to touch the reality of history and live it vicariously, that has led me to the Fehérs on this mild Melbourne autumn day.

'To me, Budapest was the centre of the world.'

Mr Fehér relaxes into a sofa upholstered in emerald green velour. His English is unexpectedly elegant and refined, so distinguished it seems almost contrived. His wife has disappeared into another room, leaving us to talk. Through the wall I hear her moving around, the sound of doors opening and closing.

'I was born in Romania, approximately five or six kilometres from the Hungarian border. My family was born in what used to be historical Hungary.'

I nod to show that I understand. I suddenly think of Mátyás, a man I knew during the early 1990s, while I was living in Budapest for a few years. The memory comes to me now because Mátyás had a map of old Hungary – he showed it to me when I visited his apartment one day. It was late winter, the trees still bare. Mátyás had offered to drive me into the hills above Nagymaros at the Danube Bend, where the river turns sharply south towards Budapest, and take me walking through the snow-covered forests there.

'*Dupla zokni,*' Mátyás said to his children that day. 'Double socks. *Kurva hideg van.*' He translated this as: 'it's very cold', too embarrassed to tell me that *kurva* meant 'whore'.

While the children were getting ready, he brought a cardboard box into the living room. Inside were the maps: six large, folded sheets, each with a number penciled on the back. We pushed the furniture to one side and he laid the sheets out on the floor in sequence, spreading his arms wide as he opened them. It looked as if he was dancing with the paper.

The floor of his living room was transformed piece by piece into Hungary at the time of the Habsburg Empire, before the First

World War. I stepped carefully around the map's outer edges, searching for landmarks among the coloured rivers and high ranges, seeking out the names of familiar towns. Mátyás ran his hands lightly over mountains and valleys, smoothing the creases of his country, pointing things out. The size of it was hard to comprehend, even though the evidence was there on the floor. The borders encompassed large tracts of land later lost, under the Treaty of Trianon signed at the end of World War I, to Czechoslovakia, Yugoslavia, Romania. Communities of Hungarians cut adrift, foreigners in their new countries.

'Nobody spoke any other language than Hungarian in my family.' Mr Fehér smiles pleasantly, remembering his childhood in Romania. His pale blue eyes are narrow and rheumy, with fleshy pouches beneath. I have the feeling that I could leave the room and he wouldn't notice that I had gone, his mind is so completely in that other time and place.

'If my mother wanted to buy a postage stamp, she had to ask someone to go to the post office and interpret for her.'

During World War II, Fehér was studying in Bucharest. Like Romania, Hungary had sided with the Axis powers. When the War came to an end, the entire region was thrown into disarray before the advancing Red Army. It was then that Fehér made the decision to move to the 'centre of the world' – to Budapest. An uncle and aunt owned a chemical factory there, they would help him get established. It was a time of upheaval, a time for new beginnings.

The 240-kilometre journey to Budapest lasted three days. From the windows of the train, Fehér saw the victorious Russians heading for home. The cries of the soldiers provided a counterpoint to the steady rhythm of wheels on tracks. *'Vojna kaput!'* they shouted, their voices falling away behind the train. 'The war is finished!'

The train stopped at the small town of Cegléd, about forty kilometres outside the capital. The connection to Budapest wasn't due for another twenty-four hours. Fehér jumped down, and started walking into town.

'Suddenly Russian soldiers stopped me. They said: *Kicsi robota*. You understand this? *Kicsi robota majelsky*. A little work. So I said: All right, I'll come with you. With a great deal of trepidation, of course.'

A freight train returning ammunition to Russia had broken down. The soldiers needed Fehér to help carry the load across the railway tracks, where a second train was waiting. Several men were already there, toiling under the watchful eyes of the soldiers. Fehér struck up a conversation with one of them, a Hungarian student about his own age. It helped to pass the time.

Suddenly, as Fehér was lugging a load of explosives on his back, he stumbled and fell. All around him, people threw themselves face down on the ground. Hands protecting their heads, they braced for the explosion. Luckily, the ammunition Fehér had been carrying failed to go off. But the Russians were far from impressed.

Fehér smiles mischievously. 'They told me to go away. In plain language – piss off! So I did what I was told.'

He thought no more about it. Until by chance, four years later in Budapest, he ran into the Hungarian student again. The young man had just been released from a labour camp in the Soviet Union.

'Yes, they took him, *kicsi robota* – they took him all the way to Siberia.'

Mr Fehér strokes a hand slowly backwards through his white hair. Somewhere in the neighbourhood a dog is barking persistently. I am absorbed in the story and fail to notice it until much later, when I play the tape back.

From time to time, he produces a large white cotton handkerchief from his pocket and dabs at his nose. There are two main types of face in Hungary: there is the round-cheeked, button-eyed type, where the underlying bones seem to have softened so that the structure is pure flesh. And there is the elegant, angular face; the shape of a long skull clear under taut skin. Fehér has the first kind of face – kindly and broad.

My father also has this face, it seems the most common. I've inherited it from him. Unusually, though, his round features – like mine – are disrupted by a strong nose. Each year as my father grows older, his face seems to recede, the flesh shrinking away from that nose. At the same time his head seems proportionately larger, compared with the rest of his diminishing body. Perhaps one day he will be nothing but nose.

Mátyás Rákosi, Stalin's man in Hungary after the war, also had a round face – the more usual kind, without the strong nose. He had a smooth, hairless cranium, thick, homely hands, and a soft chin. The flesh crinkled at his eyes when he smiled, but there wasn't any benevolence there. The long years of imprisonment he had suffered before the Second World War, for being a Communist, might have broken a gentler man. But Rákosi was a man of ambition, you could see it in the hardness of his eyes. He was a man who craved power, ruthlessly seeking it out. It was this hunger for power, more than his ideology, that gave him his strength. It gave him a reason to live. And after the War, when the Russians stayed on in Hungary – with the tacit consent of the Allies – Rákosi knew his time had come.

'I went to one of his lectures,' Fehér tells me. 'He was a very clever man. He spoke very ordinary Hungarian – he didn't speak the kind of intellectual Hungarian that most politicians speak. Of course, we didn't trust him. Nobody trusted anybody.'

The Yalta declaration of 1945 emphasised each country's right to self-determination. And so, even though Hungary was under Soviet occupation, democratic elections continued – for a few years, anyway. But behind the scenes, Stalin was quietly scheming. His plans were to eventually bring all the satellite states of Eastern Europe under the soviet one-party system. In Hungary, Rákosi helped this process along by intimidating and undermining anyone who dared to stand up to the Communist Party. These were his so-called 'salami' tactics – slicing up the opposition as easily as a roll of seasoned meat.

By 1948 the Party had virtually eliminated all other contenders, and the pace of change accelerated. Now everyone, at all levels of social and cultural life, was expected to toe the Party line or suffer the consequences. Newspapers, books and plays were all heavily censored. To further tighten the State's grip over its people, a vast network of informers developed – ordinary people who were prepared to report on their neighbours, colleagues, family and friends.

In Budapest, the university study groups that Fehér attended were guaranteed to have at least one member whose role was to report on the political interests of the others. The chemical factory belonging to Fehér's relatives was nationalised. His uncle was arrested, and interned for two years in a labour camp.

'They searched his house and they planted jewellery – they found it in his drawer although it hadn't been there before. They accused him of black marketeering broken gold.'

Fehér pulls out his handkerchief again, this time using it to wipe his brow. I wonder how hard this is for him, and worry that I might be tiring him, letting him talk too long. But we are drawing near the end now, to the time of his escape.

Despite all that he could see going on around him in 1948, Fehér believed that he could keep on with his studies and remain unaffected, as long as he stayed out of the political side of things. His group of friends was close, and he trusted them completely, to the extent where they could still laugh at anti-Communist jokes together without fear of being reported. There were frequent parties at that time, and Fehér enjoyed going to them as much as anyone else. He was enjoying his youth, making the most of being at 'the centre of the universe', and couldn't see why that might not continue.

Ironically it was at one of the student parties that Fehér finally realised he would not be allowed to stay uninvolved. He was listening to music on the wind-up gramophone when a young man he didn't know wandered over to join him.

'He asked me what I knew about a certain girl, politically speaking. Of course I said: "Nothing".'

But the young man wouldn't leave it at that. 'How about asking her how she feels about Mindszenty?'

Cardinal József Mindszenty was the head of the Catholic Church in Hungary. There was no room under the Communist system for two powerful, competing institutions, and towards the end of 1948 Mindszenty would be arrested, and sentenced to life imprisonment. But at the time of the student party he was still a free man, still a sharp thorn in the Communists' side.

'I don't like to do that,' Fehér said.

'Look, if you do it, I might be able to reciprocate that favour. And even if you don't do it, we'll ask somebody else.'

So Fehér did what was required of him. He went over to the girl. He told her: 'I have been asked to report on my conversation, and because I'm not willing to interrogate you, I'll ask you to be careful what you say.'

What happened to the girl after that, he never found out.

'These were the last days in Budapest.'

One of Fehér's friends, a journalist, was arrested soon afterwards. The Communists had discovered the journalist's name in the address book of another prisoner. Fehér grew nervous. He worried that it was only a matter of time before his own name was found in someone's book.

So he decided to make his way to the Hungarian town of Sopron on the Austrian border, and crossed at a section that was not patrolled. It was Christmas, 1948, and he was just in time. A few months later, the Communists would make the borders watertight. The country would be locked down.

OUTSIDE, THE early dusk of late autumn has fallen, turning trees and buildings into shadows. Mrs Fehér comes into the living room; perhaps she has heard that her husband is at the end of his story – the walls are thin – or perhaps she has simply sensed it. She makes tea for me and presents it formally on a saucer, the liquid a deep, rich amber, perfectly translucent in its white cup.

Mr Fehér transfers to a chair on the other side of the coffee table, and his wife sits beside me on the emerald velour sofa. They barely speak: they circle around the house like choreographed dancers, anticipating each others' movements and needs with a calm intimacy that goes beyond language.

Mrs Fehér perches on the edge of the sofa, her brown eyes large behind clear-rimmed glasses. She wears no jewellery or make up. Her voice trembles slightly – whether from nervousness or age, I cannot tell.

She was born in Sátoraljaújhely, in Hungary's mountainous northeast region, close to the Slovak border. Her father was a lawyer, and the administrative head of their town; her mother came from an old aristocratic family. Her mother's coat of arms sits above the fireplace: a framed, illustrated shield, intricate in colour and detail.

'After the Communists have taken over, people like my father were sacked from their jobs. That was the first thing.'

On a shelf near us there is a bowl filled with foil-wrapped chocolate eggs, although Easter is already several weeks past. I noticed it the moment I first walked into the room, my eyes drawn

18

to it with the tunnel vision of an addict. Perhaps it is only coincidence that Mrs Fehér offers the bowl to me now. I take an egg and peel back the scarlet foil while she continues.

Mrs Fehér's parents divorced soon after the War, and she was sent to live for a while with her grandparents in the country. Every evening, her grandfather would sit and listen to Radio Free Europe, a station sponsored by the CIA and broadcast out of Munich. The Hungarian voices belonged to free men, securely in the West, peddling an exaggerated view of the benefits of democracy. They seemed to be so near, even in the same room; and yet they were inexpressibly far away.

Mrs Fehér's grandfather used to hush the children and move up close against the radio, growing annoyed when he couldn't hear it very well.

'His hearing was perfect, that wasn't the problem. There was a background noise that was always there, made deliberately by the Comrades trying to prevent the local population from listening to the news.'

Caught between two distortions, the truth was impossible to know. At Mrs Fehér's school, where a picture of Comrade Rákosi's beaming face hung in every classroom, the textbooks had been rewritten to project a strange kind of reality. Then there was the youth organisation – the Pioneers – with their smart red scarves and rousing Communist songs. In theory at least, every child belonged to them.

'Still when I am washing up – probably I am the only one, probably everybody else has forgotten – but when I am doing something mechanical like housework, I am singing quietly these funny songs.'

The lyrics reflected the dream of socialism: people working hard for themselves, instead of putting money into someone else's pocket. It was supposed to make life better for the ordinary man and woman, but the reality was very different. Over-ambitious five-year economic plans focused on expanding heavy industry at the expense of agriculture. Labour was shifted away from the fields and into factories and mines. The result was severe shortages of essentials like bread and meat, and many household items.

One year, when Mrs Fehér was at home from university for the holidays, she found her mother using a worn out broom. She asked her mother why she hadn't bought a new one.

'Oh,' her mother said, 'I would; but for years there aren't any in the stores.'

Her daughter couldn't believe it. She trailed through the hardware shops, visiting every store in town. There were no brooms to be found.

A year went by, and once again Mrs Fehér returned home for her holidays. This time, she saw a woman walking down the street carrying a broom in her hand.

Sitting up on the edge of the sofa beside me, Mrs Fehér thrusts her arm straight out, her fist clenched around an imaginary broom handle.

'She was walking like this – so happily and proudly displaying the broom!'

Mrs Fehér went up to the woman and asked her about it.

'Yes!' the woman said. Mrs Fehér shakes the imaginary broom. Her voice is triumphant, the earlier tremor gone. 'In this and in that store,' the woman continued, 'Just got it! But go *now*!'

Mrs Fehér rushed to the shop. When she got there, she found hundreds of women fighting over the brooms. 'It was quite an achievement to actually find one or get one.' She relaxes back, lowers her arm.

In 1956, Mrs Fehér was thirteen years old. Her older sister was studying music at college in Miskolc, a large industrial city on the main rail line from their home town into Budapest. Miskolc is mostly unattractive, but the old heart of town is pretty with its churches and baroque facades. The college where Mrs Fehér's sister studied was on the picturesque main square, opposite the Town Hall.

It was late October, 1956, and in Budapest the uprising had begun. In Miskolc, an angry crowd gathered in the main square, hundreds of people milling around the Town Hall. Mrs Fehér's sister watched from a window of the college. She had a clear view across the square. The crowd swelled, and she heard people calling out the names of Party members. She realised the Communists must have taken shelter inside the building.

When no one emerged, the crowd lost patience and stormed the building. Men raced through the corridors, searching every room. One Comrade, overweight and middle-aged, was captured. They dragged him out onto the building's balcony, high above the excited crowd that was baying for his blood. Mrs Fehér's sister was close enough to see the fear in the man's face. She found she couldn't turn away, forced to watch as the insurgents pushed the man over the balcony, toppling him into the mass of people below, where she saw his body disappear in a frenzy of kicking and beating.

The girl at the window was just eighteen years old.

The strength I heard before in Mrs Fehér's voice – when she was talking about the broom – has disappeared. The tremor has returned. At first, she says, people were hopeful that the uprising would succeed.

'Well, they were very naïve – people actually thought at the beginning that they will get outside help ...' Her face reddens, she crumples a little, and can't go on.

Then she laughs bitterly through her tears, at the ridiculous optimism of the Hungarian people. I am very close to her, inches away. I want to reach out and comfort her with a touch. But I don't move. From his chair opposite, Mr Fehér watches us. His expression is calm, his legs are crossed casually at the knee.

Suddenly she straightens, seems to find her strength again.

'But it was still better than to do nothing,' she says, defiant now. 'It was still better.'

A few months after the uprising, in early 1957, Mrs Fehér's sister crossed the border into Austria with friends. Mrs Fehér was too young to try then. She waited; and in 1969, when she was twenty-five and working as a teacher, her moment came.

By then Hungarians had started travelling abroad, although they were still bound by tight restrictions. It was difficult to get a visa. Even if this hurdle was overcome, every tourist bus had a 'brick' planted among the group – someone appointed by the secret police to spy on the others and report back.

'I was the 'brick', *tégla*.'

It was a bus trip to Vienna, organised by the Teachers' Union. Mrs Fehér was uncertain whether she would be allowed to go, but she applied for a visa all the same. Shortly after lodging the application, she was visited at home by a handsome young man, roughly her own age. He turned out to be a member of the ÁVO – the Security Police, who everyone feared. He reassured her by telling her that they had gone to the same university, although she didn't remember him. They chatted for a while about their university days, harmless reminiscing. Then he got down to business.

'He explained to me that I had to watch everyone, listen to conversations; and when I came back, submit a report.'

But she had already decided that if they gave her a visa, she would not be coming back. So rather than protest, she simply went along with everything the young man wanted. After he had gone, her mother commented: 'you'll probably be issued with a visa and a passport now'. Sure enough, a few days later she was notified that she could go.

For a long time afterwards, she wondered why she had been chosen – she had never been a member of the Party. Much later, she realised that this was probably the reason why. The others in her group would have trusted her, they would never have suspected that she was the *tégla*.

They were booked into a hotel in Vienna for five days. Mrs Fehér waited until the final day. Then, when they were loading the suitcases onto the bus ready to return home, she simply walked away, leaving her luggage behind. Her heart was pounding; she prayed that no one would notice and come after her. All she had with her was a handbag and another small bag, and the clothes that she wore.

In a distraught state, still terrified of being caught, she reported to the Austrian police. They told her that she had had no choice, because she was the 'brick'. She would have been in serious trouble if she'd returned to Hungary, the secret police would have wanted their report.

Now, after all this time, Mrs Fehér is finally able to laugh about it.

'Just as well that I didn't return, because really I don't know what I would have written. Nobody did anything apart from just going with the others and looking at the sights. They didn't talk about anything mysterious. And I'm not that interested in other people's business, I'm not a very good observer.'

The chocolate Easter egg Mrs Fehér offered me is only half-eaten. The remaining pieces lie on the coffee table, nestled in scarlet foil. I don't have the appetite to finish it.

Mr Fehér brings my jacket and holds it up while I slip my arms into the sleeves. Then he opens the door for me, in the way that Hungarian men often still do. Both of them follow me outside.

When I am already a long way down the darkened street I glance back. They are standing together in the driveway, still watching. I wonder if they are trying to delay the moment when they have to go back inside, to face the memories that are now swirling through the house, suddenly alive again and uncontained. And I feel a sudden rush of guilt.

THE RIDE into town from Ferihegy airport is where it overtakes me most strongly. The feeling has been building since the twin propeller plane touched down – the first breath of crisp air, the short bus ride across the tarmac, the sound of Hungarian words all around me in the terminal. Foreign, and at the same time familiar. But it's on the minibus journey into Budapest's centre when it really hits me, as strong as ever, just like the first time: the miracle of a sense of connection, of reaching a place where I finally belong. A feeling of stomach-hollowing exhilaration, like my first skydive. I'm in freefall.

The straight route into town leads along broad Üllői út. The sun is shining. Sunlight has a different texture here compared with Australia: it's richer in colour and softer on the skin, although no less bright. Large billboards outside the airport advertise global brands with Hungarian taglines. They are like welcome signs meant to reassure: Hungary is part of the West now, you'll be safe here.

Then come the densely packed blocks of the high-rise estates. The cheerless 1960s architecture is a vision of communal living turned sour. Not unique to Communist states, but oppressive all the same, wherever they're found. The city centre draws closer; I can almost smell it. A dark tangle of tram and trolley bus wires flies overhead. Three and four storey neoclassical buildings line the road now, the ground level taken up by rows of cramped shops.

Deciphering the strange words, I pick out florists, all-night grocery stores and second hand bookshops. There is a shabby grandeur in their grimy windows and peeling facades. The plaster is mostly warm European yellow, darkened by decades of soot. The familiarity of the architecture enfolds me like a cocoon. This is where I feel at home.

The minibus drops me off in front of the apartment that I'll be renting for the duration of my stay. It's in an old building at the heart of Pest, two streets back from the Danube, facing the brown glass edifice of the Intercontinental Hotel.

I stand beside the large timber doors, and type the apartment number into the security panel. But I'm early. On the fourth floor the entry phone rings and rings, and no one answers. It's too cold to wait outside. The Gerbaud coffee shop at the end of the street, a nineteenth century wonder bedecked with draped curtains and chandeliers, offers warm refuge.

A sullen, heavy-set woman sits on duty behind the counter of Gerbaud's cloakroom.

'Is it possible to leave my luggage here?' I ask.

The woman glances down at my heavy bag. She throws me a cold stare.

'No, it's not possible.' She turns away, indicating the discussion is over. Behind her stretch shelves and racks of coat hangers, all of them empty.

'But I just wanted to have a coffee ...'

The woman sighs. 'In that case, okay.' She hefts my bag across the counter without another word. It makes me smile. There are some things here that haven't yet changed.

My hot chocolate comes served on a silver tray in a miniature cup, with a chilled water chaser. The taste is rich, with a dense cocoa flavour. At a cash register in front of the tall windows two uniformed waitresses are talking heatedly. Their postures are rigid and angry, their voices sometimes rising above a furious whisper. I try to catch what they are saying, but it's too fast and quiet, there are not enough familiar words. A third woman joins in for a short while, then all three hurriedly move away, out of sight.

It takes a long time to settle the bill because I need change, and the woman with the cash belt over her frilled white apron is slow in coming. My waitress apologises for the delay. She tells me cheerfully: 'The cashier is having a huge argument in the kitchen.' As if it happens every day.

Managing to pay at last, I retrieve my bag and leave a tip for the cloakroom woman. She rewards me with a brief, cool smile. Back at the apartment, Tibor, the owner, is standing on the street. He welcomes me in English that is easy and fluent, and doesn't seem to mind that I have kept him waiting.

Tibor is younger than I'd been expecting. He is pretty and fresh eyed, his dark hair tousled. He is dressed casually, with a daypack on his back. Tibor is young enough to have learned the languages of Europe. Young enough to have benefited from the changes. There is a woman with him, about the same age, sweet-faced and with long, blonde hair. The three of us walk inside.

A deep-shadowed courtyard lies at the centre of the building, a secret kept hidden from the street. Iron-railed balconies run around it on each of the five stories. The floor tiles are cracked, and in the dark stairwell every stone step is hollowed at the centre, where decades of residents have passed.

A small Post Office occupies the ground floor – on weekdays, the workers gather in the gloomy courtyard to smoke and chat. But today is Sunday, and no one is there. The plaster on the building's walls is grey-streaked and peeling, bruised by exposed bricks and black bullet holes, scars of the Second World War or the uprising. The second and third floors are empty. Through glassless windows I catch a glimpse of gutted apartments: large spaces interrupted by a few supporting columns, all the walls knocked through. Everything coated in pink plaster dust, pipes and tangled wiring exposed.

The woman is the one who takes me up to the apartment, operating a cramped and shuddering lift. Her English is self-conscious; she is nervous, in training. It's the first time she has shown a client around. I speak to her in Hungarian, hoping to make her feel more at ease.

'It's a beautiful day, isn't it?' Outside the sun is still shining, clear and golden despite the brisk air.

'You speak Hungarian?' She sticks stubbornly to English. 'You've been to Budapest before?'

'I lived here for a few years once.'

I have switched back to English as well, I've already given up. I don't expand – don't tell her that I came here for six months, curious about my father's country, and ended up staying for three years.

We reach the fourth floor and I follow the girl out along the balcony. She stops at a set of white double doors, with wrought iron screens protecting the glass. A small polished brass nameplate reads 'István Horváth'. The young woman turns keys in multiple locks and I step inside.

The apartment is high enough above the street to catch the sun. For a few hours each afternoon, the light floods through tall double windows and reveals the worn patches on crimson velvet chairs. It brings out the shine of brass light fittings and the glow of the polished parquet floor.

White rose-pattern lace cloths cover the tables, the bookshelves are crammed with musty hardbacks by István Örkény and Endre Ady. On a mahogany sideboard next to the television I notice a brass sextant and a sepia-toned globe. There is a faint but distinctive smell, slightly damp and musty, the scent of cool plaster. It will stay with my clothes even after I've returned to Australia, until I wash it away.

The same smell will return to me months later, in my living room in Melbourne, when I open up a map of Budapest. The watery scent entered its folds, was absorbed by the paper, while it lay on the table below the double windows in István Horváth's apartment. And with the scent's release I will see again the view from those windows: the uniform rooms of the Hotel Intercontinental, a glimpse of the Chain Bridge and the Danube flowing beneath it. The smell will bring back the grain of the table, split and worn, and the particular fall of the sun across the wood in the afternoons.

In this apartment I feel like an intruder. The old objects, the history, seem to be waiting for Mr Horváth to come back and reclaim them. It is as if he has just stepped out for a short while. We are all just waiting for a knock on the door. But everything is a little tired, a little ragged around the edges. Like a memory, already fading, of an age that can never return.

The apartment phone rings the following Sunday, late in the afternoon. I'm not expecting anyone to call. Confused and delirious with jet lag, I answer it like a sleepwalker.

'Can I speak to Doctor István Horváth, please?' The voice of a middle-aged man.

An image looms through the fog of my mind: a name on a brass plate, by the apartment door.

'He's not here.' As always when I'm speaking Hungarian, I don't manage to say exactly what I mean.

There is a pause at the other end of the line. 'But I have the right number – this is his apartment?'

'Yes, this is his apartment.'

The man doesn't believe me, seems to think I've misunderstood. 'I'm looking for Doctor István Horváth, born in southern Hungary?'

He has come across the name of his old acquaintance in the phone book, and his voice holds the hope that he might have found the Doctor again, after all these years. I give him Tibor's number.

He repeats it before he hangs up, a little less hopeful but not yet fully disappointed.

That should be the end of it, but the call stays with me for several days. I wonder about the outcome, whether two old friends managed to find each other in the anonymous city, what could have happened to make them lose touch. And the ghost of Mr Horváth is just a little more definite, a little more present, as I wander about his flat.

There are still buildings like this one, Mr Horváth's apartment block, scattered throughout the city. Sandwiched between old facades that have been spruced up to look like new. Or else dwarfed by slabs of coloured glass and polished granite, the smart banks and sprawling shopping malls. Among the gaudy, homogenous monuments of capitalism, there are still places left where there's a trace of lives lived and battles fought. Ghosts hide in the shadows of the city's reconstruction. In the serene intimacy of the narrow streets you can lose yourself, float disconnected from time.

Maps don't give you a sense of place, can't describe an atmosphere, or show you where the beauty lies. Can't locate you except in the narrowest meaning of that word. Tourists cling to maps despite their inadequacies, wanting security. They stand on street corners, poring over flat representations, always hopelessly lost.

If you look at a map of Budapest, this is what you will see: a vertical river slices the city in two. The districts, marked off with Roman numerals, radiate outwards from the centre, coloured in pastel shades. To the right of the river the spread is the greatest. This is Pest: flat, densely populated and industrial. On the left is Buda, contained by a swathe of pale green hills. The streets here curl and wind, forming interesting patterns that snake their way up steep gradients. This doesn't tell you very much at all.

30

I am searching for signs of regeneration, for a bright new country waking from the long sleep of Communism. It is what the Fifty-sixers, as the people involved in the uprising are known, fought for – democracy and freedom, the dream of a better life.

And I'm searching, at the same time, for the world described in my father's red letter. A world fifty years out of date. Wanting to discover the history, the context that might reveal the city's true meaning. If any traces of it remain.

These are things that can't be shown on a map – they will be deep in the pulse of the city, in the mood of its people, if they are to be found at all.

As I wander the streets I start to notice the changes. Glossy German cars clog the main roads now, rather than the cramped and smoking Ladas and Trabants I remember from the 1990s. The large houses winding up the hills fetch prices on a par with Brussels and Paris. My rented apartment has a rate fixed in euros rather than the local currency, forints. Jewellery and designer clothes are displayed in shop windows. An advertisement running alongside the subway escalator's handrail promises loan approvals in half an hour. So that you can have 'whatever you desire'.

But in the long queues at the local supermarket checkout, the faces still seem as sullen as when there was nothing to buy. I notice an elderly woman standing in front of the packet soup section. She peers at the products through thick spectacles, her face an inch away from the shelves. Her suit is smart, real wool, and her shoes are polished to a high shine.

'I'm looking for chicken flavouring,' she tells me as I pass. 'It's in red or orange packaging.'

Trying to be helpful, I scan the rows. The range is vast – there are delicacies like 'liver dumpling soup' and 'village-style semolina dumpling soup' – but there is no chicken flavouring.

'Perhaps this is the wrong place,' I say.

It is a world away from the shops of Communist times. Then, all businesses were State-owned and there was very little choice. Without competition, products were unappealing in their single-brand uniformity.

I head off in search of my own food. When I come back, the woman is still looking for chicken flavouring, but now she has acquired her own personal shop assistant. Together they examine a wall covered with different kinds of spices, deep frowns lining their faces.

Outside the supermarket, at the top of wide steps leading down into the subway, a man with no right arm is collecting money in a can. He sits in silence, the exposed flesh of his stump standing in place of words. It shocks me, because I don't remember seeing such poverty before.

The following day, I wander over to the Palace on the Buda side of the river, climbing high up among the cobbled streets and baroque houses of Castle Hill. From here, Pest is reduced to a flat postcard view. The eye is drawn down across winding stone stairways, to the shining grey river where Parliament sits, and beyond. The dense tangle of streets disappears, distance shrinking the wide boulevards into faltering narrow lines.

I sit on a bench over at the western side. The hills and large houses of Buda are at my back, and the courtyard of the National Gallery faces me. The trees are shedding their leaves onto the pale cobblestones, but there's a display of tall gladioli, red and yellow, still putting on a brilliant show.

I watch the people stroll past. At a nearby fountain, tourists pause to consult their guidebooks and take photographs. It is late in the season, and sometimes there is no one close to the fountain at all. In one of these quiet spaces, a man wanders up. He looks different, not a tourist: his old green tracksuit clings to his skinny legs. He wears a sleeveless camouflage jacket over the tracksuit top.

In one hand he carries a large plastic bag, its red Marlboro logo faded almost to white. His walk is tired but purposeful. Heading straight for the fountain, he puts his bag down beside it. I notice for the first time that he has a long, bent stick in one hand.

The thin-legged man sits on the edge of the fountain basin and leans precariously out over the shallow water. He starts to fish for coins tossed there by the tourists, using his stick to gather the farthest ones in. His head, with its circle of fine grey hair, almost touches the water as he reaches down. The bronze figures tower over him. They illustrate the legend of Szép Ilonka – a beautiful young woman who fell in love with a disguised King Mátyás. She died of a broken heart when she found out who her love really was, and realised how unattainable her desires were. At the apex of the statue, the King has killed a stag. Water stains stream from the animal's bronze body like rivers of green blood.

The thin-legged man has collected all the money that he can. This late in the season, there can't have been much for him to find. He wipes his hand dry on his tracksuit pants, picks up his carrier bag, and wanders away. The statue of Szép Ilonka watches him leave, her story in sympathy with his: high hopes, followed by bitter disappointment.

MY FATHER'S village can give the illusion that it is immune to change. The tourists who swarm through the hot summer streets of nearby Tokaj, swilling the famous Wine of Kings out of two litre plastic bottles, have not yet found their way here. The wine in Erdőhorváti – or 'Horváti' for short, as my father knows it – is drunk behind closed doors, cherished vintages brought out to share over conversation with visiting friends.

It is true that a swathe of concrete houses has recently sprouted around the outskirts of Horváti, expanding the village beyond its old boundaries and, in places, giving it the look of a construction site. But the streets are still unmade, clogged with flocks of geese that flap and bark as you try to pass by. The pealing bells of three churches still bring out the women on Sunday mornings, in their faded cotton dresses and tightly laced boots. They struggle up the hill, some bent almost double from years of tending the fields. Along the way they pause to greet neighbours and catch their breath, their sun-creased faces beaming toothless smiles from beneath dark headscarves. And rising above the road into the village is the cemetery, keeping the ancestors safe, the number of headstones increasing too rapidly, year after year.

Outwardly, it has changed very little since my father was here. Péter grew up on a small farm facing the bank of a fast-flowing stream. It was in this stream that he learned to catch fish using only his bare hands. Staring into the clear water, holding himself still as a rock, he studied the shadows of submerged stones. Then, seeing a sudden flash of movement, he would plunge his arm down in a rapid scoop. Occasionally he might bring up a stunned fish, but more often it was just a handful of cold water.

He tried to show me how to fish like this when I was young, in an English park near our home. Even so, it's hard for me to imagine the boy he once was, hard for me to see that boy in the man he later became. For me, the young Péter is nothing more than the story of a boy, fishing in a village with his hand in the stream. Disconnected from my father, a man who seemed to age very quickly once he stopped working, his hair grown thin and gray. His shoulders more stooped, his body more startlingly frail each time I see him. Even though he insists: 'I still feel like I'm twenty years old, no more than that.'

Still, in Horváti, the stream flows beneath the farm gates, like a kind of proof. And in the evenings the smell of wood-smoke hangs in the air, and a chorus of barking dogs disturbs the stillness. Golden lights glow warmly from kitchen windows. As darkness grows, so does the village's apparent isolation. It could be floating, cocooned from the rest of the world.

But nowhere is immune to politics or history. No place is ever overlooked.

At the outbreak of the Second World War, Hungary at first tried to take a neutral stand. This changed in the summer of 1941, when reports came through of Soviet attacks on the country's fringes. Hungary joined the Axis powers.

The dark shadow of war fell over Horváti as much as anywhere else. The healthiest young men of the village were plucked from their families and sent to fight for the Germans on the Eastern front. The Hungarian units were undermanned and poorly armed. Many of the men died in the vicious winter of January 1943 – a long way from home, in the snow south of Voronezh along the icy River Don.

Hungary's Jews became subject to discriminatory laws. Even so, for a while it looked as though they might be spared the transportations to the death camps, which were decimating communities in the countries all around. But then, towards the end of 1943, Hungary made tentative approaches to the Allies over terms for an armistice. Germany responded by sending its forces into Hungary.

The German occupation started in March 1944. It triggered major changes for all Hungarians, but especially for the Jewish population. Now all Jews were obliged to wear yellow cloth stars pinned to their lapels. And in May that year, the transportations began. The advancing Russians were drawing ever closer. So the Germans started with the towns and villages closest to Hungary's eastern border, determined to clear the region of its Jews before the Red Army could arrive.

My father remembers the day the German soldiers came to Horváti. They forced three Jewish families from their homes and herded them through the village. Twelve-year-old Péter stood with a group of his friends, watching as they passed. He was too young to fully understand what was happening; but he will never forget how one of the Jewish women turned to glare at them as she was led away. 'You'll be next!' she cried.

By late June, the rural areas of Hungary had been almost entirely emptied of their Jewish populations. In just two months, an estimated 440,000 people were sent to the death camps.

The Red Army reached the outskirts of Budapest towards the end of that year. Now, in a final desperate act of genocide, the Nazi Arrow Cross began liquidating those Jews that still remained within the capital's crowded ghetto. Hundreds of people were lined up along the Danube's bank and shot, their bodies swallowed by the icy river.

The Germans had orders to make a stand in Budapest, rather than simply abandon it to the Russians. As a result, the fighting went on through most of that winter, and left much of the city's architecture in ruins. It wasn't until April 1945 that the last of the

German troops withdrew from Hungary. Then a new phase of occupation began.

After the War, raging inflation made money worthless. Péter's family survived on the milk and eggs they produced on their farm, and bread made from ground meal. They chipped black salt from blocks of rock, and boiled sugar beet for molasses. A large barn was built in the village, to store produce collected under the quota system. The food was transported away by truck to feed the Russians, while Hungarians starved. It was the price of their 'liberation'.

The tobacconist at the centre of the village had only a few packets of cigarettes to offer. They looked sadly incongruous on the otherwise empty shelves. Next door, the general store that used to sell bicycle tyres, hardware and tools was closed for a long time. The owner was one of the Jewish men led away by the Germans, and he never returned. His shop was eventually taken over by someone else. When it reopened, the only product it had to sell was pig meal.

There were rare days of excitement, too, when word got around that food had arrived. Once, it was sugar. But when Péter opened his bag he found the white grains vibrating, alive with ants.

At my parents' house in Scotland, where they live now, the forest comes down to meet the garden. They like to take walks through the trees. On their walks, my father will point out mushrooms to my mother. He knows the different varieties, which ones are poisonous and which can be eaten, easily recalling both their Hungarian and English names. He has become something of a local expert on mushrooms – his neighbours will often ask his advice on specimens they have picked.

In his back garden, my father plants vegetables. He has a large plot of land set aside for it, and rotates the crops every year to keep the soil fresh and the yield strong. There are potatoes, carrots, cabbage and red onions. In a greenhouse, he nurtures tomatoes and capsicum. There is more than enough to feed the two of them. Enough to keep them alive, if it ever came to that.

But in the front garden my father plants flowers, hundreds of them, creating a display of vibrant colour that lasts almost all year round. He takes photographs of the flowers – pansies, chrysanthemums and roses – and posts the pictures to me. He spends a great deal of time in this part of the garden, pruning, seeding and trimming. It's a luxury, to spend so much energy growing plants with a value that is purely aesthetic. A luxury that, these days, he can afford.

In 1953, when my father turned twenty, his call-up papers arrived. Péter found that first year of compulsory military service the hardest. He had to learn what was expected of him, and get used to being away from home. To start with, there were three months of training at an air force base in Kunmadaras, on the vast and desolate Hortobágy plain.

Puszta, the Hungarian word for the plain, translates as 'bleak' or 'deserted'. On the Hortobágy puszta, flat, swampy grasslands stretch to infinity beneath a low, windswept sky. There are no hills, rocky outcrops or tall vegetation to provide a rest for the eye. What few buildings exist are visible from great distances: small, whitewashed stone farmhouses, Artesian wells towering beside them like unbalanced crucifixes. They are a reminder that there is some kind of living to be made on this land. But these houses, and the occasional small town, are adrift on a featureless sea, at the mercy of bitter winters and the relentless wind.

The winter of 1953 was one of the harshest on record. Snow settled up to a metre deep, and temperatures fell to minus 32ºC. Night after night, the new recruits were forced out on walking exercises across the snow-covered puszta. The ground they marched on glowed silver in the moonlight, beneath a star-speckled sky. Without trees to break its path, the fierce wind tore across the land, hurling ice into Péter's face. Underneath the snow the earth was frozen solid, jarring his legs as he walked.

Even for my father, raised in the country and used to extremes of weather, the exercises were almost impossible to bear. Pain shot through his legs at every step. His boots seemed to be made of lead, and he was barely able to lift them from the ground.

The late hour, the rhythm of his paced marching, and the monotony of the landscape combined to produce in him a hypnotic, dream-like state. Glimpsed through a haze of drifting snow, the distant horizon seemed to shimmer and shift, echoing the mirages that were known to appear on the puszta in summer. The biting wind pierced him to the bone. Out there, even with the other men around him, he felt utterly alone. Human life seemed insignificant, compared with the vastness of the plain.

The end of the training period was marked by a swearing-in ceremony, held out in the open at the airport. It was a bitter January day. The recruits stood in line beside the runway as they waited to sign their names.

For Péter, this was worse than the night marches across the puszta. At least the strenuous exercise had generated warmth, and helped to keep the blood flowing. Now they were forced to stand perfectly still, forbidden even to stamp their feet or rub their hands together. There was no way of protecting themselves from the cold. It easily pierced the fabric of their uniforms, seeping under their skin and laying icy fingers on their bones. Péter's muscles trembled uncontrollably. His teeth chattered in his skull.

Then, along the line from him, one of the soldiers collapsed. He was carried inside. A second man fainted. Another followed, and then another. The ink they were using to sign with froze solid in the bottle, so that also had to be taken inside. Péter, the hardy country boy, was one of the few left standing right to the end.

Nine months later, Péter was transferred to an air force outpost at Ligettanya, a place too insignificant to appear on any map. It sits on the eastern reaches of the Great Plain, not far from the Ukrainian border. His job there was to guard the base, which held an underground storage depot for aircraft fuel.

The work was not difficult or physically demanding, but the three years of his military service seemed to last an eternity. Péter yearned for home. He longed to be back with his family, helping out on the farm – especially in autumn, when he was needed in the vineyards to harvest the grapes. His leave entitlements allowed him to return to Horváti from time to time, but those breaks were never long enough.

The ache was constant. It affected him most strongly at night, or when he was alone on guard duty, with nothing else to fill his thoughts. Gazing out across the bleak emptiness of the puszta, he would try to impose over it images of the forested hills around his village.

Finally, at the beginning of October 1956, his three years came to an end. He was impatient to get home before the weather turned to winter. But strangely, no replacement soldiers arrived to relieve him. Péter knew he could not be mistaken about the dates – he had been counting down the days. So he waited.

October slipped past, and still no relief soldiers appeared. This was the first sign that something was very wrong; but as yet Péter didn't understand it.

The second sign reached them a few days later. A loud, deep rumbling noise shook the base, the earth literally trembling from it. The roaring sound travelled easily across the flat landscape. It came from the direction of the main road, four kilometres away, and continued relentlessly for several days.

The soldiers at the base listened in horror. Now they knew what was happening. There was no mistaking the roar of Russian tanks, vast numbers of them, pouring into the country across the Ukrainian border. The main road ran straight across the plain towards the capital. It was the fastest route from the Soviet Union into Budapest.

UPRISING

Molotov Cocktails

IT IS WINTER in Melbourne. A bitter wind gusts across Federation Square, chilling me to the bone even though the sun is strong. The treeless, rose-tinted ground swells and rolls beneath me like natural waves of earth.

The SBS radio offices are here, housed in one of the stark new buildings. Inside, the décor is industrial grey and dimly lit. Only the friendly receptionist provides a little warmth. I am here to meet Tony Ámon, the Melbourne presenter for Hungarian Radio.

Earlier, I looked up Ámon's photograph on the website, and I'm expecting a man with a long, heavy beard. When he comes to greet me I fail to recognise him. Unlike the picture, his chin is clean-shaven, although he still wears a bushy, grey moustache that threatens to eclipse his mouth. The sleeves of his red plaid shirt are rolled up, displaying strong arms. An image comes to me of traditional horsemen galloping across the Puszta.

Ámon leads the way into the depths of the building, along a labyrinth of grey corridors. The studios sit behind heavy glass doors, pregnant with banks of glowing switches and dials. His workspace, when we reach it at last, is cluttered with papers and books. Across the partition a group of people are speaking a language that I can't begin to recognise.

Ámon is a cautious man. He doesn't tell me anything of his story on our first meeting. He wants to see me first, to find out who I am, see how serious I am. He needs to be sure of my intentions. And then he needs time to collect his thoughts, to decide on exactly what he will say.

By our second meeting, Ámon is ready to share what he remembers. He has also prepared a list of people I might want to talk to, migrants who came out of Hungary following the uprising. The names, in double columns, fill more than two pages.

We find a studio where we can talk privately, and squeeze into the tight space as best we can. Ámon has noted a series of events on a sheet of paper, and he refers to this as he talks, ensuring he covers them all. He is a man who likes to make lists.

Leaning over the desk, he sketches for me the layout of his family's old apartment block in Budapest. The building in Józsefváros, Budapest's VIII district, no longer exists – it was demolished some years ago to make way for modern apartments. The old building used to stretch back from the street, its shape long and narrow. The family's flat, where Ámon lived with his younger sister, his parents and grandparents, was at the front, on the first floor. The windows faced the street, overlooking a button factory on the opposite side of the road.

The VIII district today is still a maze of narrow streets and passageways, just to the east of the city centre. It was in this congested residential area that some of the fiercest fighting of the uprising took place. Ámon was only eleven at the time, but he remembers it well. He feels it was the defining moment of his life.

'I would say that the first rhythm, as the uprising started,' Ámon tells me, 'was *Ruszkik Haza!*' – Russkis go home.

His voice is suited to his job: resonant and soothing, the pace measured. He takes time to order his thoughts before speaking. On the desk beside us is a screen displaying a large clock. The seconds are ticking down. Ámon stares off to one side, his eyes focused on the distance as if he can see the past unfolding there.

'And the concluding rhythm would be: *Három lépcső, fejre vigyázz!*'

Three steps, watch out for your head.

As a boy, Tony Ámon was fascinated by the statue of a First World War soldier in Harminckettesek Square, a busy intersection near his home. The soldier, from the local 32nd Regiment, is frozen in the act of hurling a hand grenade. His right arm is raised, drawn far back behind his head, ready to begin the trajectory of the throw. The soldier's left leg lunges forward for balance; the left hand grips a rifle with its bayonet attached, the sharp tip pointing up to the sky.

The statue is full of movement, even though it stands perfectly still. On 23 October 1956, a Tuesday, eleven-year-old Tony also stood transfixed. He gazed up at the green-streaked man, examining the face obscured by shadows beneath the round helmet. A walrus moustache was the only clear detail. At home, Tony had a collection of tin soldiers which he arranged into armies, setting up battles for them to fight.

It was early evening, and the smell of frying *lángos* filled the square. The day had been mild, unusually so for the time of year, and a gentle warmth still lingered in the air. A restless crowd milled around the boy as he stood in front of the statue. Tony's mother was queuing nearby at a restaurant window, waiting to buy *lángos* for the family's tea.

Tony realised that there were more people than normal in the square that evening. Young and old, they were wandering animatedly about in the fading light of dusk as if it were New Year's Eve, or as if they were at some kind of fair. Their voices were raised in excitement, and Tony sensed their agitation. His mother came over to him, carrying her *lángos*. But instead of returning straight home with the fried dough, mother and son stayed on in the square for a little while, absorbing the atmosphere of exhilaration that seemed to electrify the air.

Later that night, back at their apartment, they heard the first shots fired in the darkness outside.

'I just didn't comprehend anything,' Ámon says. 'But the adults in our home were very excited about it. And sometime afterwards we were put to bed. Or at least, my mum tried to put us to bed. The excitement had sort of grafted itself onto us – onto myself, and my five-year-old sister.'

Tony lay awake, unable to sleep. Strange noises floated up from the street below. Late into the night, people were walking up and down outside the window, their voices and footsteps echoing along the narrow street. The traffic was heavier than in the daytime, trucks trundling past over the cobblestones. The men on the trucks shouted out a single, rhythmic slogan:

'*Ruszkik haza! Ruszkik haza!*' Russians go home!

The same phrase repeated over and over, like a lullaby urging him into sleep.

Tony's school was in Prater utca, just around the corner from their flat. But over the next few days, his mother wouldn't allow him to leave the building. Their four rooms became suddenly claustrophobic, and Tony was drawn repeatedly to the forbidden area of the large front windows, overlooking the street. He would stand with his face pressed up against the glass until the adults chased him away.

'Every morning, the first thing was to look at the building opposite and check whether there were any new pockmarks in the wall, from the splinters and shooting. It was always very exciting to find a new thing in the mortar surface!'

Because in the streets outside, his toy soldier games had miraculously come to life. The vivid images that passed through his narrow field of vision during those few days would always remain with him. Men and women carrying rifles walked up and down the street. Once, a Red Cross lorry passed slowly beneath his window. People covered with blood were crowded on its platform.

'And it was very early on – I remember, it was a sunny morning – I peeped out towards the telephone exchange corner.'

The district telephone exchange was on Mária Terézia Square, a kilometre or so to the north of the Ámons' flat. The Communists had occupied the exchange building. They were defending it against a group of freedom fighters.

'People were walking with arms ready in the street, from one door recess to another, approaching the square. And I saw a tank coming into my view, and stopping. Then a man, wearing a canvas raincoat and a beret, jumped up on that tank. He was immediately shot down by the Communists in the telephone exchange. He fell down.'

Tony, firmly on the side of the freedom fighters, was devastated by the man's death.

Then, in the last few days of October, the fighting stopped. The Russian tanks began rolling out of the city, in retreat. It seemed that the revolutionaries had won a miraculous victory. People returned to the streets in their thousands. Everyone wandered about gazing at the damage. It was as if they needed to see the evidence of the struggle with their own eyes, before they could allow themselves to believe in its success.

Tony also ventured out, staying close to his father's side.

'We saw Russian soldiers, covered with whitewash to disinfect. And burned out vehicles. And rubble everywhere, damaged houses all over the place.'

I have seen the photographs taken during that quiet period, and the shaky documentary footage. They are arresting images, in stark black and white. Russian tanks and armoured cars, burned out and abandoned, lie scattered across the roads. Buildings stand ripped open, bricks jagged around the wounds, the intimacy of the apartments inside exposed. Rubble from crumbled walls is everywhere underfoot.

And there are the bodies that Ámon is talking about. Russian soldiers lying in the street where they fell, their corpses dusted with white lime. Beneath the disinfectant their faces appear smooth and boyish, not very much older than Tony would have been. In their uniforms and capes, they look like children in fancy dress who have fallen asleep, exhausted after playing a wonderful game.

JÁNOS DABASY, wearing the black robes of a Lutheran pastor, is on stage in front of a large crowd. His height and size give him a commanding presence. The ecumenical service is in Hungarian; but this is Wantirna, in Melbourne's eastern suburbs. The church and community centre that local Hungarians built for themselves, brick by brick, nestle among tall pines. It is their refuge, the language and culture of the homeland preserved.

With an assured confidence, Dabasy assists the congregation through the practised rituals. At the end of the service, the people stand as one to sing Hungary's national anthem, the Himnusz. The majestic rhythms swell, filling the community centre's hall. I search for the words on the hymn sheet, but they are not there – there is no need. Everyone except me knows them by heart.

A week later, I meet Dabasy at his home. He is dressed in a casual shirt and trousers, in shades of soft grey. His physical stature is not diminished, but without the formal black robes he seems more approachable. His large, fleshy mouth widens in a smile. It takes in the whole of his round face, dimpling his cheeks with a look that is mischievous and innocent at the same time. He is youthful, vivacious; yet there seems to be a trace of sadness in his eyes.

Although perhaps I have added that with hindsight, after hearing his story. Perhaps I only imagine I saw it there.

'The congregation only exists because of the Hungarian language,' Dabasy says.

We are sitting on cream coloured sofas in his airy, tranquil living room. A classical music station plays on the radio – he has turned the volume down so that we can talk. Through large windows there is a view over rooftops to blue, rolling hills.

'Otherwise they could go to the Australian churches.'

But the congregation is growing old. The liturgy used is from the 1930s, familiar and safe. The children of the original migrants, born and raised in Australia, don't have a good enough command of Hungarian to properly follow it. For the Church, time is running out.

The Communist régime in Hungary frowned on the Church, but that did not stop Dabasy from following his religious beliefs. His father had been a major in the old Royal Hungarian Army, and because of this Dabasy was already classified 'X' – an enemy of the working class. He had nothing to lose. As a boy in the town of Győr, he attended a school run by Benedictine monks. Then he was offered a place at Budapest's Technical University, where he went to study engineering.

But during his student days in Budapest, Dabasy was hiding a secret. People with the classification 'X' were not allowed to go to university – he was not supposed to be there.

Then how did he get there?

For the first time, I sense a reticence in Dabasy. He is uncomfortable discussing the origins of this 'mistake'. While at school, Dabasy had submitted his application for university, certain that it would be refused. The application had to pass through multiple layers of bureaucracy – his school in Győr, the local education department, the district education department, and then eventually Budapest.

'And by the time my application arrived in Budapest, my classification was changed.'

He wants to skate over it, I have to press him for more detail.

Initially, Dabasy himself had no idea what had happened. Then, during his university course, he undertook some standard military training. While there, he was able to sneak a look inside his own file. There it was, in black and white. He was no longer an enemy of the working class.

Much later, Dabasy discovered that somewhere in all the red tape of the application process, his forms had happened to cross the desk of a friend of his. The friend had changed Dabasy's classification, and in so doing put his own life at risk.

'I have never told anyone who that person was,' Dabasy says. 'And I am not going to tell anyone, despite the fact that he is already dead.'

And finally I understand why Dabasy has been so reluctant to talk about this. The fear can outlast the régime, carried like a parasite in the minds of those who lived through it. For Dabasy, it will never really be over.

Dabasy's college rooms in Budapest were within the Castle district – the Vár – on the Buda side of the river. The large residential building stood a stone's throw from the ornate and beautiful Mátyás Church. It is still there today, among immaculate baroque houses on a cobblestoned square, opposite the grand white façade of the Hilton Hotel.

But in the 1950s, the Castle district was a different kind of place. Heavy fighting at the end of the War, as the Germans retreated, had destroyed many of the historic buildings. During the years that Dabasy stayed there, the Vár was a wasteland of rubble and ruins, mostly deserted, a deathly quiet place.

'Practically a ghost town.'

But Dabasy was happy there. He had relatives in Budapest: an aunt who lived with her two daughters. During the week, Dabasy would have dinner at the college, in the communal dining room. But on Saturdays, when there were no classes to attend, there was also no cooked meal in the evening. Instead, at lunchtime, the college provided sandwiches. Dabasy would sometimes slip the sandwiches into his coat pocket, and head out for the afternoon to visit his relatives.

The moment that he walked through his aunt's door, he would be greeted by his favourite cousin, sixteen-year-old Márta.

'You couldn't have dreamt of a nicer, more beautiful little girl.'

Her dark hair swinging behind her, Márta would rush to meet Dabasy. She liked to jump up and put her arms around his neck, then plant a kiss on each of his cheeks. At the same time, she would manage somehow to slip her hands into Dabasy's coat pocket, feeling for the sandwiches she knew to be there. Then she would run laughing from him, clutching the stolen food.

For the sake of the game, Dabasy pretended to be angry with her; even though the smell of the dinner that his aunt was preparing would usually already be scenting the air.

As well as having his relatives close to him, there was another reason why this was a happy time for Dabasy. He had met and fallen in love with a young woman. Her name was Bea, and they were engaged to be married. It was sheer luck that had got him a place at university; but now he was there, the future seemed clear and promising, without further surprises. Dabasy could not know that a further twist of fate was on its way, one that would mean he would not complete his studies. He could not know that it would tear him and Bea apart.

In the autumn of 1956, Dabasy had commenced his third year of study. On Monday 22 October, he remembers that a meeting of all the students was called in the Technical University hall.

'There was something in the air,' Dabasy says.

This is an understatement. There was a restlessness in Hungary, and some of the other satellite states, that had been brewing since

Stalin's death from a brain haemorrhage – or possibly poisoning – three years before.

With the dictator gone, the Kremlin was plunged into a prolonged battle for the leadership of his empire. Initially, the tide of opinion appeared to turn against Stalin's oppressive rule. In Hungary, Rákosi was forced by Moscow to give way to Imre Nagy, a leader far more moderate and balanced in his policy. Nagy's 'New Course' brought in several popular measures of economic reform. Political prisoners were granted amnesty. The head of the despised Security Police, Gábor Péter, was arrested and sentenced to life imprisonment for his crimes against the country and its people.

But Nagy's leadership did not last long. The power struggle in the Kremlin continued, and so did the instability. Moscow considered that Nagy had pushed his reforms too far. In 1955, Nagy was first relieved of his post, and then expelled from the Party altogether.

Rákosi regained some of his former power; but now he faced strong opposition within Hungary. Nagy had shown what was possible, and many Hungarians were reluctant to return to a tighter régime. In February 1956, Khrushchev, the new Party leader in Moscow, delivered a speech that was heavily critical of Stalin. This encouraged the Hungarian Writers' Union and the intellectual Petőfi Circle to grow increasingly outspoken in support of political reform.

At around the same time, László Rajk, a charismatic and high-ranking Communist executed in 1949 – on the strength of a forced, false 'confession' – was rehabilitated. This meant that his name was finally cleared. On a blustery day in early October, Rajk was reburied with full honours at Budapest's Kerepesi cemetery. The reburial became a symbol for reform, and two hundred thousand people turned out for it. By this time, Rákosi had been dismissed from his post as First Secretary. He left Hungary for Russia, never to return again.

Meanwhile, in neighbouring Poland, First Secretary Gomulka was pressuring the Soviets for greater independence. Polish students mobilised in support of their leader, staging demonstrations.

There was something in the air, then. With hindsight, it might be seen that the region was in a volatile state, and a single spark would ignite an explosion.

But at the time, as Dabasy points out, no one anticipated anything of the kind. The purpose of the meeting at his university that Monday was simply to discuss the events in Poland.

Dabasy's face glows as he describes the mood in the packed hall. Everyone was excited, energetic.

'It was amazing.'

Always conscious of his precarious position at the university, Dabasy was cautious about fully giving in to his feelings. But beneath his anxious restraint, he was secretly rejoicing.

The fierce political debates and discussions went on late into the night, the students never tiring, everyone eager to have their opinions heard. They decided to hold a demonstration the following day, Tuesday the 23rd. It would consist of a march through Buda to the statue of the Polish General Bem, who fought with the Hungarians in the revolution of 1848. The driving idea was still to show support for the Polish people.

As the first freely organised demonstration during eight years of Communist rule, it was a bold enough move. But during that long night, the students went further still. They came up with a list of demands to bring increased independence for Hungary as well.

There were sixteen points.

Foremost among them was a call for the Russians to leave the country, and withdraw their occupying troops. There were also demands for free multi-party elections, and the release of political prisoners.

As the meeting finally reached its close, the students discussed how they could make multiple copies of their sixteen points, so that they could be distributed during the march. The university had a Roneo duplicating machine, but access to it was strictly controlled. Under Communism even typewriters had to be registered, to prevent the production of materials critical of the régime. But the students were not deterred. They broke into the room where the Roneo machine was kept, and ran off hundreds of duplicates of their demands.

The following morning, the students gathered behind the iron gates of the university courtyard. Despite his fears for his own situation, Dabasy had decided to join them. The march started out in the afternoon, and headed slowly northwards through Buda, towards the Polish General's statue at Bem Square.

Across the river, students from the Eötvös Lorand University had also organised a march. Theirs started from the Petőfi statue in Pest. It would follow the eastern bank of the Danube as far the Margit Bridge, and then cross over to Bem Square to join with the others.

The weather was fine and bright, warmer than usual for the time of year, a golden and glowing autumn day. As the students walked along, they handed out the duplicated sheets of their sixteen points. They gave them to bus drivers, passed them in through the windows of trams. Workers and those living along the route, or people simply passing by, became caught up in the mood of cheerful excitement. They joined the marchers. The numbers quickly swelled.

'We went to the statue in Buda, and from there, in the evening, we went across to Parliament. And by that time we had met up with all the other students and demonstrators, so the square in front of Parliament – well, that was packed with people. I don't think you could drop a pin and it would fall on the ground!'

Budapest's Parliament building sits on the embankment on the Pest side of the river. Its neo-Gothic architecture and central cupola echo London's Houses of Parliament. The open square in front of the building is named after Lajos Kossuth, leader of Hungary's 1848 revolution against the Hapsburg empire. The demonstrators completely filled the vast square. Everyone was chanting slogans.

'It was just a dream,' says Dabasy now. 'It was just a dream coming true.'

The demonstrators began calling for Imre Nagy, the former prime minister who had introduced reforms following the death of Stalin. One of the demands on the students' list was that he should be returned as prime minister. The people crammed into the square in front of Parliament took up the cry: 'Imre Nagy! Imre Nagy!'

'Personally, at that time I didn't actually like Imre Nagy,' Dabasy says, 'because he was still a straight-out Communist. But all that said, he was a Hungarian first and a Communist second. And eventually he paid for it with his life. So you have to respect that.'

Now Dabasy's memory falters a little, after almost half a century. He remembers that Nagy did eventually appear, a round man with a heavy walrus moustache, and he spoke to the crowd in Kossuth Square. He doesn't recall the details of the speech.

'But as for what he said, I took it with a grain of salt, because I didn't trust him. He was still of Communist ilk.'

He struggles to remember what happened next. The people in the crowd were determined to make their demands heard, but there had been no fighting, no scuffles, and no one was armed. The police had chosen not to interfere. There was not much they could have done against such large numbers in any case.

'Then we were fired on.'

Dabasy is unsure about the timing, whether the firing started during or after Nagy's speech. In fact, the history books do not record any shooting in front of Parliament that night. Dabasy seems to have confused it with another demonstration that took place two days later, on Thursday 25 October, also in Kossuth Square.

On that other day, the demonstrators gathered in the morning. Everything was peaceful until the shooting started suddenly, without any provocation or warning. It was around eleven o'clock. Dabasy must have been there as well, and in his memory the two separate occasions have concertinaed into one.

'The secret police had taken up positions around the buildings in the square, on the top floors,' he says, 'and they opened fire on us from up there.'

On that Thursday, the square was again jammed with people. None of them were armed. When the volley of fire broke out, everyone immediately scrambled for shelter. But in such a crowd, the casualties had to be high. Around a hundred protestors were killed outright that morning. Many more were wounded.

Some of the survivors fled to the American Embassy, just around the corner. The photographs show them pressed on the street in front of the Embassy doors, faces disfigured by shock and anger, pleading for the Americans to send help.

But on Tuesday night, October 23, the shooting did not start at the demonstration in front of Parliament. It started a few kilometres away, at the Radio building in Bródy Sándor utca, nestled behind the National Museum. While Nagy had been speaking in Parliament Square, another group of demonstrators had gathered at the Radio. They crowded into the network of narrow streets behind the Museum, clamouring to have their list of demands read out over the air.

Dabasy's memory becomes clearer now. At Kossuth Square, Nagy had delivered his speech from a balcony of the Parliament building, and disappeared inside. It was late, but the crowd did not disperse. Everyone stood around feeling vaguely dissatisfied. They had not heard the rousing words they had hoped for – Nagy had been noncommittal, failing to deliver the promises that would have matched their heightened mood. But they were at a loss over what to do next.

Then news filtered through that something was happening at the Radio. The square started to empty. Some people went home; others headed for Bródy Sándor utca. Dabasy, with a few of his student friends, decided he was not yet ready to go back to the college dormitory. They made their way through the dark, cobbled streets towards the Museum. They had no idea of what awaited them there.

The Radio was being guarded by a detachment of ÁVO men, the Security Police. The ÁVO were armed with rifles. The demonstrators, although unruly and passionate, had no weapons of any kind. The buildings of the radio complex sprawled across a whole block, but the demonstrators were concentrated around the front entrance, in Bródy Sándor utca. People were packed in tightly, there was no room to move. When the ÁVO started shooting into the crowd, there was no place to shelter, nowhere to run or hide.

As Dabasy and his friends drew near to the Radio they heard the sound of gunfire, loud and continuous.

'I saw a truckload of Hungarian Army soldiers – who were sent out to quell the revolution – refusing to fire on the Hungarians. And they were handing their armaments, their guns, over to the demonstrators.'

The demonstrators were fighting back. The spark of ÁVO gunfire had caused the inevitable explosion – the uprising had begun.

Dabasy realised it would be too difficult and dangerous to get any closer to the Radio. He doubled back and went to check on his fiancée, Bea, who lived with her family nearby. Once he had made certain that she was all right, he went back out onto the streets. He had decided to try and return to his lodgings, on the other side of the river.

By this time, it was the early hours of the morning. The warm day had deteriorated into a bitterly cold night. Dabasy reached the Chain Bridge. He found a Russian tank blocking it. The tanks of the locally based Soviet troops had rolled into Budapest during the night, and had taken up strategic positions throughout the city.

A group of students were gathered around the tank on the bridge. They were talking to the Russian soldiers, and Dabasy went over to join them. He was close enough to touch the cold side of the tank. Using the Russian they had been forced to learn at school, the students were describing to the soldiers what had happened during the night. The soldiers seemed sympathetic. They had been stationed in Hungary for some time. They had made friends, and the country had become like a second home to them.

It was clear that the Russians were not about to start shooting anyone, so Dabasy continued on over the bridge and up the hill to the Vár. When he reached the college, many of the residents were missing. He thought they were most likely still in Pest, fighting the ÁVO. Dabasy went to his room and tried to get some sleep, suspecting he would be grateful for it later. When he rose the next morning, the sound of gunfire could still be heard clearly, floating across the river from Pest.

'And that's when it happened,' he says quietly. 'A death in my family.'

That morning, Tuesday 24 October, Dabasy's aunt and his cousin Márta were visiting friends in the centre of Budapest. Their friends' apartment was close to the Radio. Outside, the heavy fighting had continued through the night. The sound of gunfire was too much for the irrepressible young Márta to resist. Excited, curious to see more, she was drawn to the apartment window. From there she had a good view out onto the street. But those in the street below could also see her.

'Someone may have thought that she is a demonstrator,' Dabasy says slowly. 'And thought she may use a firearm from there.'

Up at the Vár, the students were organizing themselves into guard units, and Dabasy was kept busy for several days. It was only towards the end of October, once the Russians had withdrawn and things seemed to be settling down, that he visited his relatives to see how they were.

His aunt opened the door.

'I knew immediately it was something really bad.'

There was no Márta rushing to greet him. There were no mischievous hands thrusting into his pockets, checking for sandwiches. Only his aunt, dressed in black, her eyes raw with grief.

Márta had been looking down onto the street, framed by the window, when she was shot. A single bullet found its way to her throat. The aim of it too precise to have been a stray.

Just off the Múzeum körút, not far from the Radio, there is a small green oasis bound by iron railings. This is the Károlyi kert. It backs onto the courtyard of Count Károly's former palace. The winding pathways of the peaceful garden still draw in local residents, it's still a place where young lovers can be found embracing on benches, where parents bring their children, and the elderly wander slowly through, breathing the fresh air. It's a place to escape all the noise and pressures of the inner city.

During the uprising everything stopped – the cemeteries were closed, and materials for coffins were difficult to find. So this is where sixteen-year-old Márta was buried, at the Károlyi kert, in a box fashioned from wooden doors.

ISTVÁN PÁLOS sits perched on the edge of the armchair in my living room. The plate of biscuits I have put out on the table is untouched. I had offered to talk to Pálos at his home, thinking he might feel more comfortable there. He said he preferred to come to me. He explained his house was quite chaotic, that there was nowhere suitable for us.

Perhaps this is true. But perhaps it is some more of the caution, concealed in old-world politeness, that I had noticed in Tony Ámon. Possibly Pálos wants to find out more about me; and at the same time prevent me from discovering too much about him, other than what he is prepared to disclose. In his place, I would probably do the same.

Pálos is dressed neatly in a neutral coloured pullover and trousers, and smart boots that look new. He has a long, lean face. His dark hair is swept back from a high, domed forehead, and he strokes his full beard thoughtfully from time to time. Only his hands seem out of place: the thick palms and short, stiff fingers make them appear too heavy for his slender body.

'Going back to that summer of '56,' Pálos says, 'I can't say we were absolutely ignorant of the situation. Somehow, we felt something. But you asked if we knew what was going to happen – absolutely not! Absolutely not! Because of the fear that all the people had. You couldn't even cross the street in the wrong way, because the police would brutally stop you.'

Pálos speaks very softly. He gives the impression of a calm, gentle person. But there are also hints of a strong core of determination. His large hands are more expressive than his voice. With wide, sweeping gestures, he draws pictures in the air. Then he takes his glasses off to talk, as if he can see into the past more clearly without them.

In 1956, Pálos was working as a mechanics assistant at a medical instruments workshop in Buda's XI district, not far from the transport hub of Móricz Zsigmond körtér. He was eighteen years old, and had completed his diploma at the technical high school only that summer. This was his first real job.

Pálos started out with a vice and file, making small parts for dental instruments. Like most factories, it was piece work – the more you produced, the more you could get paid. Pálos quickly learned how to make the parts faster and more efficiently. By his second week he was already earning reasonably good money, especially for his age.

Early in the morning of Tuesday 23 October, Pálos was at the workshop as usual. The wireless was on. In between the music came news of a march planned by the students to the Petőfi statue. It was announced that the Minister of the Interior, László Piros, had banned the march.

The workshop was not far from the Technical University. A little before nine, Pálos's friend Dezső, who was studying at the university, dropped by. He was in an excited mood, and eager to tell Pálos about the student meetings that had been held the night before, and the plans for the march.

'I thought this person must have been crazy!' Pálos says. 'I was looking around – where is the police? It was an absolutely unheard of thing!'

Pálos and Dezső had been friends right through school, sitting next to each other in the classroom. Dezső had an unusual condition – his nose bled very easily. This had worked to the boys' advantage in the past, getting them both out of a few unpleasant situations. Most memorably, it had helped them avoid the commemorations for Stalin's death, three years before.

When Stalin died, everyone had been required to gather in Sztálin Square, a large parade ground at the edge of the city, to pay their respects. It was a sunny, warm afternoon. Thousands of people were pressed into the square. Just before the official proceedings were due to begin, Dezső's nose started bleeding profusely. Immediately, the two boys were escorted out through the cordon of police, to the nearest tram. From there, they made their way home. Pálos smiles as he recalls that the tram was crowded. The boys were not the only ones who had managed to wriggle out of their obligations that day.

'Well, the march is on,' Dezső told Pálos. 'Whatever they said. And you will hear us come.'

Early in the afternoon, Pálos did indeed hear the marchers outside, heading towards the city centre along Bartók Béla út. There were about ten men at the workshop that day. Every one of them, Pálos included, downed their tools and went out onto the street. From shops, apartments and workplaces all along the route, people were flooding to join the march. It was suddenly much more than just a student demonstration.

In those initial minutes, before the numbers swelled beyond control, there was a strong sense of danger – the fear that the Security Police would arrive and start arresting people.

'You were not logically thinking. Well, there were people who were logically thinking – they didn't come! They watched us from the windows of their houses.'

The march continued up along the river embankment, past Gellért Hill and the Szabadság Bridge. By now, the street was crammed with people of all ages. Flags in the national colours – red, white and green – had begun to appear. People waved them from balconies and apartment windows. Some of the flags had gaping holes at their centre, where the Communist emblem had been ripped out. Each time one of these appeared, it was greeted with great cheers from the crowd. People were chanting slogans, and singing the Marseillaise.

'From the beginning, you were leaning outside of yourself. If you were yourself, you maybe couldn't do it because of the fear. You know, it's amazing, but I still remember the feeling. How sometimes you remember a taste, or a smell? You sometimes remember a condition of yourself on that moment.'

Continuing on through Buda along the river, the march passed the Chain Bridge and eventually arrived at Bem Square. The small square filled quickly, people pressing around the statue of the Polish general, his left arm raised, pointing the way, a plume in his hat. There wasn't enough room for everybody. Pálos was too far back to see or hear anything, but word rippled through the crowd that demonstrators at the statue were reciting the poet Sándor Petőfi's words: 'Arise, Hungarians! Shall we be slaves or shall we be free?'. Petőfi had declaimed this poem in the spring of 1848, a rousing cry to revolution against the Hapsburg monarchy.

It was now late afternoon. Some of the marchers began to make their way across the river, heading for Parliament. Pálos decided to join them. The warm day had turned overcast as evening drew closer, and the crisp bite of autumn was in the air. A cold wind blew off the Danube. As he crossed the Margit Bridge to Pest, Pálos felt the chill through his threadbare winter coat, and pulled it tighter around himself.

In front of Parliament, Kossuth Square was already filled with people. Everyone stood shoulder to shoulder in the gathering dusk. The singing continued, and the shouting of slogans. Streetlights blinked on; the dark mass of Parliament towered over the restless crowd. Then the red star mounted over the building suddenly lit up, illuminating the sky. Immediately, a new slogan ran through the square: *'Oltsák el a csillagot!'* Extinguish the star! And they called for Imre Nagy.

'We wanted Imre Nagy. He was a devoted Communist, don't worry about it; but he was a human Communist.'

It was the most that the protestors could dare hope for – a shift in the régime towards something more human, a slight relaxing of the system. It was still, at this point, unimaginable to demand the end of Communism altogether. But Pálos is in no doubt about the mood of the crowd in the square, about what people really wanted.

'These days, they want to put the revolution up as purifying the Communist system – that's absolutely not true. I never knew anybody who was a Communist before, who came to us and said: "All right, I'll fight with you because I want a better Communist system". They were all hiding. The revolution was absolutely anti-Communist.'

In Kossuth Square, the demonstrators continued to shout their slogans. There were still no signs of movement from within the Parliament building, and no officials had appeared. Then, without warning, the streetlights went out. The square was plunged into total darkness. Only the red star remained alight. But if this action was intended to disperse the crowd, it failed.

All around Pálos, people began to pull newspapers from their bags. They rolled them up and struck matches to set them alight, as makeshift torches. Pálos himself did not have one. 'I never read newspapers, because they were all propaganda.' But most of the people in the square seemed to have bought the paper that day, perhaps in the hope that it would contain news of the demonstration. As the idea caught on, more and more bright points of flame appeared. The light spread rapidly across the vast, black space.

'Thousands and thousands and thousands of lit newspapers in the square!' Pálos's face is radiant with the memory.

Shortly afterwards, the streetlights came back on. At the same time, the red star high above the square went out, to the delight of the cheering crowd. A spotlight appeared on one of the lower balconies of the Parliament building, and someone came to announce that Imre Nagy had been sent for. But it was much later, around nine o'clock, before Nagy finally stepped onto the balcony. He was met by an outburst of clapping and loud cheers from the demonstrators below. Unfortunately his very first word shifted their mood.

'*Elvtársak!*' he said. 'Comrades!'

Immediately, an enormous clamour and whistling broke out among the crowd. '*Nincs elvtárs!*' they cried in response – 'there are no Comrades here!'

Nagy collected himself. His button eyes peered out from behind his round rimless spectacles. Then he tried again, addressing the crowd as 'fellow citizens and friends'. This time, he was allowed to continue. He spoke for perhaps ten minutes, no more than that. The only promise he made was that he would discuss the situation at a Central Committee meeting the next day.

'He didn't say very much, probably out of fear; or else he didn't know what was happening himself. That was the good thing about it, that's how it escalated so fast, because nobody knew what was going to happen – not even the officials or the Security Police. Maybe Moscow was still too far away at that time, they didn't have instructions.'

After finishing his brief speech, Nagy disappeared inside. The crowd stayed on in the square, chanting their slogans.

'I'm not sure what we wanted. I'm not sure. There was still a lot of excitement.'

Then a truck came barrelling out of a side street. There were a dozen people hanging from it. The men called out: 'Go to the Radio! They're shooting people at the Radio!'

Pálos didn't believe it. In front of Parliament things were winding down. He couldn't believe that anything more would happen that night.

'I thought they were some sort of activists from the other side, just wanting to get the people worked up.'

Pálos thought of his elderly father and sister. They would be at home, waiting anxiously for him. In the Second World War, Pálos's elder brother had gone away to fight, and had never returned. Pálos's father, because he had waited in vain before, understood what could happen. With every passing minute, he would be growing more and more convinced that he had lost another son. Pálos knew he had to go home.

His family lived in the southern suburb of Budafok, about eight kilometres from the centre of Budapest. Because of the demonstration there was little public transport. Throughout the city, trams stood empty in the middle of the streets, abandoned by their drivers. Pálos began walking.

The Radio happened to be on his route home, and Pálos decided to look in as he passed. He was still some way off when he heard a sound like distant fireworks, cracking and popping in the night.

'That is when I started to believe that it happened.'

He kept walking, drawing closer to the source of the noise.

'I wasn't a brave person, never – I was always a cautious type of person. But at that time I never felt fear or anything like that. It was more excitement, and curiosity – what's happening?'

As Pálos crossed Üllői út, he noticed that the streetlights were off. By now, the sound of gunfire was extremely loud. Pálos reached the corner of the Museum gardens and Bródy Sándor utca, the street that led to the Radio buildings. He couldn't get any further. The narrow street was in total darkness. People were spilling out of it.

The night had turned very cold, and there was a dampness in the air. On the corner of Múzeum körút, burnt-out ÁVO trucks and military vehicles littered the road. Among them was a single disabled tank: an old Russian T34, an ex-war model of the kind still in use by the Hungarian Army. Earlier, one of the people in the crowd had disabled it with nothing more than an iron bar. The bars, as thick as a man's thumb, were used by tram drivers to operate track points. They were carried as standard equipment on every tram. The insurgent had thrust the bar into the caterpillar tracks of the tank.

'Being an oldish, Second World War type tank, one of the caterpillars broke. And if one side of the tank breaks, it's disabled, because it can only go in circles with the other track.'

But an iron bar was not much use against the machine guns of the Security Police. All around Pálos, people were saying, 'What do we do? We need to get guns.' Some of them climbed onto trucks. They wanted to head off in search of weapons.

Up to this point, Pálos had been simply a curious observer. He had stood apart while the action happened around him. Now, he had a choice to make. He could stay where he was, watching as events unfolded, and then return home to his anxious father. He could have waited out the rest of the revolution in the safety of his home. Many people did. But at that moment, Pálos made an irreversible decision. He jumped onto one of two trucks that were just leaving, and rode it out towards the industrial suburbs of Pest.

Throughout our conversation, Pálos tells me repeatedly: 'I am not a hero, I am not a fighter. I was just there!' But with that one choice he made the transition from observing into acting. He became a part of the revolution, a cog driving the wheel. And from that moment on, there could be no turning back.

It was already well into the early hours of Wednesday morning. The road was shrouded in fog. The trucks slowed almost to a crawl in those places where the fog was most dense. Riding out on the back platform of the truck, Pálos heard an ominous rumbling. It seemed to come from several kilometres away. It was the sound of

70

Russian tanks, their chains grinding over cobblestones. They were heading for the centre of Budapest.

The trucks began zigzagging to avoid the main road. They did not want to risk running into the Russians. Because of this and the fog, the journey took a good hour. When they finally arrived in the northern suburb of Újpest, it was not yet daybreak, but it was light enough to make out the houses by the side of the road. Here, in one of the side streets, somebody said there was a police station where weapons were stored.

The two trucks turned into the street, with Pálos on the second vehicle. This turned out to be his good fortune. Because the moment that they entered the small street, they came under heavy automatic gunfire. With no weapons themselves, they couldn't return the fire. There was no choice but to retreat. The leading truck turned around, and both made it back to the main road. But in that short time, half a dozen people from the front truck had been badly injured. They transported the wounded men to a large light bulb factory close by, where they could be looked after. Then Pálos rode back into the city.

The truck dropped him off at Keleti railway station. It was seven or eight in the morning, and completely light now. There were people everywhere – office workers, students, factory workers with their lunch bags under their arms. Pálos saw a tram conductor with his conductor's bag on one shoulder, and a rifle slung across the other.

Pálos's exhaustion was catching up with him after the long night, but he wandered through the streets, keeping an eye out for weapons and ammunition. When he came across some rifle bullets, he slipped them into his coat pockets and continued on.

The Russian tanks had reached the city some time ago, and had taken up positions at most of the major intersections. On one street corner, Pálos ran into a group of them. The soldiers were standing idly about on the cold, damp pavement. The grey early morning light showed their guns clearly. Pálos still had the rifle bullets in his pockets.

He hesitated. They had seen him, he was sure of that – it was too late to turn around.

Then a civilian walking just ahead of him was stopped by the soldiers. They began to search the man for weapons. A small scuffle developed. While the soldiers were distracted, Pálos edged slowly backwards. He reached a nearby gateway, and slipped through without anyone noticing. Now he was safe, out of sight.

Pálos is relishing his story, and clearly enjoys having me as an attentive audience. He jumps out of the armchair and strides about my living room, acting out the sequence of events. He pats his imaginary coat pockets, showing where the rifle bullets were kept; and creeps slowly backwards across the rug while invisible soldiers are distracted. He has also slipped from English into Hungarian. As fully absorbed as he is in the story, I'm not sure he even realises that he's made the switch. I don't want to disturb him, to break the spell he is creating. I follow along as best I can.

Unsettled by the close encounter, Pálos took the bullets from his pockets and hid them in the street. He thought he could always come back to pick them up later if he needed to. By then he was starving as well as tired, having not eaten since the previous day. A cousin of his lived nearby – she worked as a doctor at an institution for the mentally ill, and her husband was a bank official, so they were reasonably well off. Pálos went to their apartment, hoping to get some food.

The couple was shocked when they opened the door to find Pálos standing there, exhausted and covered in dirt.

'What are you doing here?' his cousin asked. 'Are you hungry?'

'Of course!' Pálos replied.

His cousin made him something to eat. Pálos remembers the wonderful sensation of having a full stomach at last. He remembers feeling warm, and stretching out on a bed. He doesn't remember much else after that.

A long time later, Pálos woke up. He was astonished to discover that it was already Thursday morning. Eighteen hours had simply disappeared. Pálos had been tired, certainly; but he found it hard to believe that he had been asleep for so long.

'It was the 25th, and I told my cousin I have to go home. There was no telephone, we couldn't send a message to my father – he would be worried, could have a heart attack.'

Pálos set out on the long walk back to Budafok. Russian tanks were in position on the bridges over the Danube, but they were letting civilians through. At Móricz Zsigmond körtér, not far from the medical instruments factory where Pálos had been working when it all began, several tanks were occupying the square. The körtér was the terminus of the suburban train service out to Budafok. To Pálos's surprise, the train was still operating part of the way. He took it as far as he could, and then walked the rest of the way home.

His father, who had already lost one son to a war, couldn't hide the tears in his eyes when the dishevelled Pálos appeared at their apartment door.

When Pálos finishes speaking, it is late. On the table beside the armchair, his coffee has grown cold, a skin of milk congealing on the surface. He picks it up and drinks it quickly, explaining: 'I do this all the time at work as well'. Becomes so focused on what he is doing that everything else recedes. This intensity, and the contrast with his gentle manner, is one of the first things I noticed about Pálos. The evening has brought it out more clearly still.

The central heating clicked off about an hour ago, and I shiver in the hallway as I show Pálos out. He promises to return in a week's time to continue the story – there is the second Russian intervention, and Pálos's escape, to come. The night gusts in through the open door as he leaves, chilling the hallway even more. The house is suddenly silent and still.

ROUGHLY EIGHT kilometres south of present day Budapest, heading out along the Balatoni út, the road first climbs and then swerves suddenly into a sharp S-bend. The traffic has to slow to negotiate the curves. From the final bend, glimpsed through trees on the hillside, the city is spread out below. The view draws the eye towards the Buda hills. On the eastern side of the road lie the cobbled streets of the XXII district. The ground slopes away, the large old houses becoming smaller and more crowded in together as the streets run down towards the banks of the Danube. This is Budafok, the area that gentle-mannered István Pálos once knew as home.

Two kilometres further south along the Balatoni út is another place I have come to see. The Statue Park, a strange memorial to the Communist years, occupies a flat, cleared area of land. Pálos wouldn't recognise it, although some of the park's contents might be familiar to him. The large, dark sculptures are visible from some distance away. A muscled sailor strides forward with a determined gaze. Soldiers and workers hold flags aloft. It is the land of the giants, a graveyard for socialist-realist monuments ripped from Budapest streets after the end of the régime.

One hot summer afternoon in 1992, before the park opened, I drove out here with a few friends. Many of the statues were already in place, scattered across a wasteland among mounds of earth and new bricks. We wandered around the perimeter of the construction site, taking photographs through diamond-shaped gaps in the wire fence.

More than a decade later, despite the neoclassical brick entrance and the rough gravel paths that wind through scrubby grass, the place still has an unfinished feel. An extensive parking area is deserted. At the entrance kiosk, a scratchy recording of old revolutionary songs is playing, and I picture Mrs Fehér back in Melbourne, singing as she washes her dishes at the sink. The statues look abandoned, their imagery more extravagant when stripped of the context of streetscape or an audience. And a tall wire fence still encircles the compound – as if, even now, someone is afraid that the statues might escape.

In the centre of Budapest, on the broad, tree-lined avenue of Andrássy út, another legacy of Communism has been turned into a museum. I walk out from the city past the opera house, towards Heroes' Square. Stately nineteenth century apartment buildings tower over me. Some of the facades are darkened with pollution, the brickwork worn. Others are freshly renovated. The avenue is a memorial – to the golden years of Hungary, before the First World War ripped away its territories and power. But the four-storey, dove grey building at the corner of Csengery utca holds a different kind of past. It's one that some would prefer to forget.

Number 60 Andrássy út is the House of Terror. The name is stenciled in a contemporary black fascia that runs along the roofline. During the Second World War, the Hungarian Nazis used this building as their base. Then, after the German retreat, the Communist Security Police moved in. Through the worst of the Stalinist years, it was a building that Hungarians feared. Friends, neighbours and relatives would be picked up in the middle of the night, and transported here in black cars. Most people knew at least one person who had disappeared through the doors of number 60 and had never come out again.

The queue for tickets reaches past the door when I arrive, but this is a quiet day. When the museum first opened, it could have gone either way – would people want to remember, or would they rather forget? In the event, the organisers need not have worried about their investment. The magnitude of the response went far beyond what anyone could have predicted. Day after day, week after week, the line of people waiting to get in stretched far along the street. Hungarians queued patiently for hours for the chance to see inside.

In the entrance hall, haunting, funereal music sets the mood. Two imposing granite headstones stand at the top of the stairway, one black and the other red. The black headstone commemorates the victims of the Nazi Arrow Cross movement; the red one is for those murdered by the Communists.

The orchestra strings surge, then die away. The composer is in his twenties – too young to have experienced the worst of the Communist years. The schoolchildren wandering out through the lobby are also far too young to remember. Still, they are strangely quiet, subdued by the memories of previous generations.

Inside, a light-filled square atrium lies at the heart of the building. Most probably this was once an internal courtyard, open to the sky. A mud-splattered tank rests on the ground floor. Around and above the tank, the walls of the atrium are lined with black and white images of victims' faces – row upon row of them, soaring three stories high. There are so many that when I try to focus on any one individual, the picture seems to shift and blur, the features merging with its neighbours. Some of the people, especially the women, appear to be smiling gently. It makes me wonder how the photographs came to be here: whether they were stolen from family albums, or taken surreptitiously, the subjects happy and unaware.

The designers of the museum clearly want it understood – their work is to respect the memory of those who suffered, not sensationalise the horrors of the past. The House of Terror opened just before the 2002 elections. Some argued it was a political stunt, designed to build anti-Communist feeling. If it was a ploy to get the right-wing government re-elected, then it failed.

The radio presenter Tony Ámon had told me that the two most important pillars of Hungarian life are politics and history. With an English commentary playing over my headphones, I negotiate the labyrinth of rooms on the second and first floors, and find plenty of both. The Nazi occupation, the Gulag, deportations and persecution. On the first floor is the corner office of Gábor Péter, former director of the Security Police. In Nagy's easing régime of 1953, he was arrested himself – being a high-ranking Communist could sometimes be a liability rather than a protection.

Leaving the final room on the first floor, I step into a lift that sinks gradually down a black shaft to the cool damp of the basement. The slow descent into darkness is unnerving. It gives me the sense that I may not return.

Set into the smooth, cold stone of the basement is a row of thick wooden doors, with heavy iron bolts. A line of electric lamps runs above the cells, providing a harsh light. Some of the doors are open. In one cell, the ceiling is so low that it is impossible to stand upright. Another is shaped like a vertical coffin, so that standing would be the occupant's only option. In a third cell, two inches of cold water cover the concrete floor.

Just beyond the narrow corridors of the recreated cells is the hall commemorating the 1956 revolution. The exhibit that absorbs my attention is the black and white newsreel footage, playing on monitors set into a central display. There is vision, but no sound.

I watch, fascinated, as men in trench coats and caps wrench cobblestones from the street and stockpile them for ammunition. A street sign – 'Lenin körút' – lies broken and trampled on the ground. People are walking everywhere, in the absence of trams. Freedom fighters in long belted raincoats stand smoking on street corners. Others, rifles slung across their shoulders, climb over captured Soviet tanks, their faces lit by the jubilance of the early days.

Then there is the footage of the devastation caused by the Red Army. The camera tracks silently through wet, damaged streets. Rubble lies across tram rails. Buckled wheels and pieces of burnt out trucks are scattered across the pavements. A balcony hangs loose from the side of a building. The apartment behind it is ripped open, displaying the pictures on the walls and the patterned paper that covers them. Pieces of wood jut from the broken buildings, their ends smashed like matchsticks.

The camera pans across endless lines of women queueing in the cold for food. A man slowly pushes a bicycle weighed down with bags and clothes. A middle-aged woman runs along a deserted street wet with rain, her face distorted by fear.

Oblivious to time and the movement of people filing past me, I stand and stare at the jerky, sometimes blurred images, watching as the tapes circle around, endlessly repeating.

By the time I emerge onto the street, it is late afternoon. The light is golden. The pavement cafés on Liszt Ferenc tér by the Music Academy are crowded with cheerful students and tourists. I think how extraordinary and wonderful it is that my memories of the city are mostly good ones. How magical it is to wander the streets without fear, unassailed by sudden waves of darkness. It makes me feel almost guilty.

In the early 1990s the restaurants, bars and late night streets of Budapest were overflowing with expatriates, journalists and accountants, cashed up and intent on having a good time. All of us plunderers, making the most of an opportunity that might not come again. Yet the journalists were mostly harmless, paid to observe and comment, not to intervene. The accountants were the mercenaries – hired at top rates to usher in the new economy, smoothing capitalism's way. We got our hands dirty with privatisations, foreign investment, overseeing the use of western funds.

One of my earliest jobs in Hungary was the audit of a glass factory in Salgótarján, a northern border town. I stayed there through the week, returning to Budapest only at weekends. I did not enjoy Salgótarján. Compared with Budapest, I found it a bleak and featureless place, forged from grey concrete. It was a place that seemed to have been born out of Communism, and which was now stuck firmly in that era. The focus of the town was the glass factory, where much of the population worked.

On my first day, I walked the length of the cavernous building that housed the heart of the factory – the regenerative tank furnace. It was like walking through a Bosch painting, a dark and flickering industrial hell. The building, three stories high and the length of a battleship, was airless and windowless. The sheer scale of it rendered electric light ineffectual, bathing everything in permanent twilight.

The intense heat settled on my limbs like water, slowing movement and thought. The heavy air bore the tired, bitter taste of iron. The sound of this hell was glass shattering, over and over, the clamour drowning any attempt at speech. I watched men in blackened overalls working near the mouth of the furnace. Their job was to shovel slivers of broken glass onto conveyor belts, which delivered the fragments into the flames to be melted down again. Some of the men were shirtless, their sweat-soaked skin glowing amber in the dim light.

The boardroom we worked in that spring was away from the main factory buildings, cool and peaceful. A dark bust of Lenin watched over us, dust softening its angular features. We pored over payroll printouts, turnover figures and supplier invoices under his gaze. In the executive dining room we ate lunches of *főzelék* – lentil stew – with a group of visiting Japanese businessmen. The machinery was outdated, unable to compete in western markets.

80

The factory, still in State hands, needed foreign investment to survive.

When I grew tired of the financial records, the reams of pale green computer paper, I would leave the boardroom and wander through the workshops, on the pretense of gathering information. I asked a lot of questions, but not all of them were the kind I was being paid to focus on.

In one room, I came across women slicing sheets of glass into smaller rectangles for picture frames. They leaned over their work with rulers and cutting tools, forearms gliding across the smooth surface, carving patterns like skaters on ice. One of the younger women wore leather cuffs that stretched from her wrist to her elbow, but the others' arms were bare.

I watched their rapid, graceful movements, their deep concentration.

'Do they sometimes cut themselves?' I asked.

'Only when they're new,' the supervisor replied. 'They get used to it after a while.'

The process of manufacturing glass was fascinating to me. I followed the trail of molten glass as it emerged from the furnace in a glare of white-hot liquid, and was drawn steadily upwards through the factory floors. Rollers flattened it into a broad ribbon, which cooled as it rose. By the time it reached the highest level of the building, it was already firming and transparent. Workers cracked the glass ribbon as it emerged through the floor, and lifted it in great sheets from the machinery.

I learned that the solidity of glass is an illusion, that the atoms lie in random disorder even when fully cooled. It is vitreous, a liquid with special properties, the flow of it so slow it is imperceptible. The changes can only be seen in retrospect, over time – as in the windows of medieval churches, where a fragile, brittle top thickens towards the base.

In a country also, the changes do not appear while you are there and watching. They only become obvious when you leave for several years, and then return.

THE AUSTIN Hospital, on its busy Heidelberg corner site, is bathed in fluorescence in the dusk. A glowing beacon on the hill, it seems to be signalling to Melbourne's luminous office towers, ten kilometres to the west.

The poorly lit streets of Heidelberg Heights also reference the City. Swanston, Collins, Flinders, Spencer – a roll call of the central grid. But the houses that line the streets are run down, paint peels from their dull facades. The gathering darkness seems to hold within it an undertone of threat. Here, in the shadow of the hospital where he has worked for most of his life, Sándor Tóth lives with his wife and their six children.

The single storey house has a good-sized front yard. Two old, rusting vehicles are parked on patchy grass. A teenage boy opens the door when I press the bell. He leads me in a circular route via a cramped kitchen to the living room. The most direct path – the hallway – is blocked by a table piled high with clothes and bolts of fabric. Plastic bags stacked on the floor are crammed with more of the same. The Tóths run a stall selling clothes at the Hungarian Community Centre most weekends.

In the living room, Sándor Tóth is leaning comfortably back on a sofa. He wears old tracksuit pants, and a sweatshirt that emphasises the protruding curve of his belly. He has a soft, round face and merry eyes.

Apologising for the clutter, Tóth waves me distractedly into a seat. The room is filled with an eclectic jumble of furniture, all of it well used. A fish tank sits beside the television, a framed picture of a girl in a graduation gown stands nearby. The first place I choose to sit – a sofa – is comfortable but too far away from Tóth. I move to a chair that brings me closer, but it creaks and rocks alarmingly under my weight. I try to sit very still.

Without waiting for me to pull out my notebook and tape recorder, Tóth launches into a rapid-fire monologue. He will keep this up long into the evening, barely pausing even to draw breath.

'First of all, it wasn't a revolution. It was an uprising. Revolutions were always started by conspirators, and as far as I am concerned, they are just criminals. If you have an argument against government, head into politics and argue there through legal channels, avoid all the bloodshed. What took place in Hungary was sudden and unexpected.'

This seems like a good start, but I soon realise that the trajectory of Tóth's speech is as chaotic as his house. He darts randomly among subjects as diverse as current Australian politics, the job of nursing, and the state of his father's feet.

'He was five years in the war in Russia,' Tóth says of his father. 'He came home with frozen feet. He came out to Australia when he was eighty-three years old, and he was still treating his feet. The skin and the flesh peeled off his body all the time, there was no cure for it.'

As the evening goes on, Tóth becomes ever more animated, caught up in the drama of his story. He leaps from the chair several times to illustrate certain points – the size of a sandbox, the way to carry a rifle so that it is ready to fire. My questions and attempts at direction bounce unnoticed off the barrage of his words. I am forced just to listen, and change the tape from time to time.

Tóth's children come and go while he talks. Some he breaks off to introduce, and some of them he ignores. I learn that his eldest son, also named Sándor, will be getting married in October. When the slight, fresh-faced Sanyi enters the room, Tóth berates him fiercely.

84

'You ought to have a shave, young man – I've said it to you many times. Getting married like that! If I was a girl, I wouldn't give you a kiss at all!'

Most of the family has retreated to the kitchen to give us an opportunity to talk, but Mrs Tóth appears regularly to offer coffee and plates of biscuits or cake. A shy, self-effacing woman with a warm smile, she persists in speaking English for my benefit, even though she is uncomfortable with it. And at some point, two small boys creep into the room, unnoticed by me at first. They sit up close in front of the television, watching the movie *Grease* with the sound turned low.

'I wanted to be a detective.'

Tóth had done some work after the War for his local police station in Kőbánya, an industrial suburb of Pest, and had got to know most of the staff there. He had also undergone rifle training and shooting practice.

'I was always crazy about rifles.'

But in 1956, Tóth's dream was still some way off becoming a reality. He was working in a dried noodle factory in Ferencváros – Budapest's IX district – as a maintenance man. He was twenty-one years old.

On Tuesday 23 October, Tóth was at the smallest of the factory's three plants in Ferencváros. As at István Pálos's workplace across the river, the radio was on. Tóth heard the news of the march – first, that it had been banned; and then, about an hour later, that the ban had been lifted. The march would take place after all.

Tóth didn't pay much attention.

'I wasn't interested in all this sort of thing. It was done by university students, mainly.'

He finished up at two in the afternoon, and took the tram home to Kőbánya through the brilliant sunlight, just like any other day. Within half an hour he was at the local sports club, where his brother played top-level handball. The clubhouse was a social focus for the young people of the district, whether they played sport or not.

That afternoon at the clubhouse, Tóth ran into his friend István.

'There's something big going on in the city,' István told him. 'Do you want to come and have a look?'

'I heard it on the radio at work,' Tóth replied. 'I don't know what's going on – some kind of march.'

He still wasn't particularly interested. István, however, felt differently. He was eager to find out what was happening.

'All right,' Tóth said at last. 'Let's go in and have a look.'

The number 28 tram from Kőbánya rattled past the high grey walls of Kerepesi cemetery before veering off to the left. It deposited the two young men at the intersection of Rákóczi út and Lenin körút, in the city centre. As soon as they got off the tram they could see that broad Rákóczi út was crammed with people. The crowd flowed from the direction of the Danube out towards Keleti railway station. At first, Tóth simply stared in amazement.

'There were thousands and thousands of people jam-packed. There were middle-aged people as well by that time, not only students. There was a lot of working-class men, and young tradesmen like myself.'

Some of those in the crowd called out to the two men as they passed: 'Come on, you working class boys – come and join us!'

Tóth and István did not need any further persuading. They worked themselves in among the thick throng of marchers and walked with them up the wide road. The march passed the imposing arched glass frontage of Keleti station, and continued on towards the city's outer edge.

'There were all kinds of slogans being shouted: Where is the Hungarian uranium? Freedom for Hungary, Russians out of

Hungary. And everything else along with it. The general public was going hot and mad!'

At Dózsa György út the crowd took a left turn, heading for the Városliget – the City Park. At the western edge of the park was Sztálin Square, with its wide, flat procession ground that stretched for several blocks. Official Communist rallies and marches were held there on holidays and special occasions, soldiers parading sixteen abreast in front of their smiling Party leaders. Here also was an eight-metre high bronze statue of Stalin, mounted on blocks of pink marble.

The statue depicted Stalin in military uniform, his trousers tucked into heavy boots. On his massive head, stylised waves gave an impression of flowing hair. The bronze to make it had come from the melted-down statues of historical Hungarian figures.

'By the time we got there, there was anything up to 200,000 people already assembled. Where they come from, I don't know. But they were all there!'

In the fading light, Tóth could see that some men had climbed up on the statue. They were trying to pull it down with ropes. The ropes were attached to several trucks, which had gathered around the statue's base. Tóth and István edged their way through the mass of people. They managed to get right up against the statue's marble plinth.

On one side of the square were the buildings that held Party offices and union headquarters. Tóth noticed the curtains in the windows moving. They were being watched. But the officials stayed inside, none of them daring to interfere. The crowd was too animated, the numbers too overwhelming to be controlled.

The men who had climbed up onto the statue were using oxyacetylene torches to slice into Stalin's shins. Fiery sparks glanced off the bronze. Tóth recognised one of the men as a worker at the shipyards, and guessed that the cutting equipment had come from there. But even with the torches, progress was slow.

Finally, Tóth scrambled up himself. He helped pull steel ropes around the statue, to try and topple it. But the ropes weren't strong enough. They snapped under the strain. Then a heavier steel hawser was found, and handed up. The circumference was as thick as a man's arm. Tóth helped thread this around the statue, binding Stalin's hands.

With the hawser secured, the ends were passed back down to the waiting diesel trucks. The trucks revved their engines, pulling the rope taut. The statue towered over them, solid and immoveable. It wore the ropes like decoration – a necklace and bracelets made of steel. The trucks' wheels screeched as they turned uselessly on the concrete, their burning rubber tyres sending up clouds of bitter smoke.

Then someone called out: 'Come on, every one of you – up onto the trucks! Put weight on the trucks!'

Tóth and István jumped up. There were around thirty men on every truck.

'Right, let's go now! Get the trucks moving, and pull it!'

The engines started up again. The statue hung in the balance for a moment, the hovering shadow of a giant.

'And then it came down like an atom bomb!' Tóth's eyes are shining.

Only the dictator's boots were left, standing empty on the marble plinth.

I have held a piece of the Stalin statue in my hand, an irregular chunk small enough to sit neatly in my palm. I have felt its weight, and marvelled at the unexpected heaviness. One of the edges was lightly scored with fine lines, made perhaps by the tool that shaved it from its home. The other surfaces were smooth and dark but, as I turned it, the room's lights awakened a soft, golden gleam. I passed the bronze on around the table, heard the reverent whispers as it moved from hand to hand: '*Sztálin szobor, Sztálin szobor.*'

It was 23 October 2003 – the anniversary of the day that Stalin's statue was brought crashing to the ground.

Gentle-mannered István Pálos was there that night. He read out a poem he had written several years before, describing the things he saw during the uprising. It was somber and melancholy, but ended with a hopeful tone.

His friend László Budaházy had come to the commemoration as well. Budaházy made his way up to the microphone, leaning heavily on a cane for support, and talked about a monument to the freedom fighters built recently in his and István Pálos's home district of Budafok. Then, in a powerful voice, he read out a list of names of the dead. Thirteen of them in all from his district – two women and eleven men.

Afterwards, over a meal of goulash soup with bread, I listened as they reminisced, swapping fighting tales. I imagined them telling the same stories to each other year after year, cementing them in their memories, as a way of reminding themselves that it really happened. That they had been a part of it. Both Pálos and Budaházy have children, but not one of them was there that night. None of their children had ever been interested enough to come. I watched those elderly men, and wondered: Who will take up the storytelling once they are gone? Who will be left to understand the significance of a palm-sized sliver of precious bronze?

At Sztálin Square in 1956, the crowd celebrated the fall of the dictator's statue. The atmosphere of intense emotion had reached dangerous levels. Everyone present in the square that evening felt it – there could be no turning back from here. There was the feeling that now things had to change.

Then news filtered through to the crowd of a speech that the Prime Minister, Ernő Gerő, had just given over the Radio. Gerő had announced that a fascist mob had assembled in Sztálin Square. Euphoria transformed into a hot, furious tide of anger.

'Up onto the trucks!' came the cry. 'Let's go to the Studio!'

All around Tóth, people were attacking the statue with picks and hammers, breaking off pieces for souvenirs. But Tóth had lost interest in the felled dictator. He wanted to be where the action was. Jumping onto a truck, he rode back along Rákoczi út, towards the Radio buildings.

LÁSZLÓ BUDAHÁZY and his fiancée, Suzanne, were also in Sztálin Square that night. People were packed into the square so tightly that it was hard to see what was going on. László lifted Suzanne onto the concrete base of a streetlamp, five feet above the ground, to give her a better view over the heads of the crowd. She was there for more than an hour, watching as the trucks strained on the ropes, trying to bring the statue down.

'It just wouldn't budge,' Budaházy says. 'And everybody was just waiting for some miracle.'

The soft-voiced István Pálos had given me Budaházy's phone number, but warned me that his friend was inclined to be 'grumpy'. On the day that I called, Budaházy answered. I explained who I was. His voice was strong and fierce.

'We had a car accident at the weekend,' he declared abruptly.

'Oh, no! Was anyone hurt?'

'We are all right. But the car is not.'

'Perhaps this is not a good weekend for us to meet, then.'

'No – you can come on Sunday.'

There was the faint sound of a woman's voice in the background. Budaházy turned away from the phone. I heard him say, in Hungarian: 'I'm not going to church! I don't have a car.'

We arranged a time for Sunday. But before the weekend, he called to switch the date to Saturday afternoon. 'I will pick you up from the station,' he said, his tone gentler than before. The car had turned out not to be so badly damaged, after all.

It is the day of the Australian Rules Grand Final, and the streets are eerily quiet. Everyone is at home, watching the match on television. I have a whole carriage of the train to myself. I get off at Broadmeadows, in Melbourne's northern suburbs – the end of the line. The houses continue on: new estates slowly engulfing the rolling hills and pasturelands around the city's edge, spreading ever further outwards. There is a bus from the station, but the service stopped running at midday. There will be nothing now until Monday morning. This is why Budaházy offered me a lift.

Their small car is parked outside the station. I notice the Hungarian tricolour on the rear window, and climb inside. I sit in the back and Mr Budaházy drives, while his wife in the passenger seat beside him makes gentle conversation. Fifteen minutes later, we reach the tidy cul-de-sac where they live, and Mrs Budaházy leads me inside. Her husband follows a short time later, walking with difficulty, after closing up the garage.

We settle slowly around the dining table in the open plan living area. A piece of clear plastic covers the table. Over it is draped a large tablecloth of white crocheted lacework, with a delicate floral pattern. It makes me think of Hungary – the decorative doilies hand-made by my aunt in Erdőhorváti; the chair and table coverings in old Budapest apartments; the tablecloths held up for tourists by the line of elderly women that always stands along Váci utca.

László Budaházy sits at the head of the table, to my right. Behind tinted glasses, his left eye is squeezed permanently shut. The good eye is blue and a little rheumy. But his hair is thick, and his fine features are clearly defined. There is a sense of power in his voice, as well as in the way he carries himself. If it wasn't for the cane that he relies on to stand or walk, you might think he was in his late fifties – in fact, he is seventy-two. It is as if he has resisted the process of ageing through sheer strength of will.

Suzanne Budaházy sits opposite her husband, her arms resting on the table. Her eyes are bright, and her expression is open and friendly. She tucks her hands inside the sleeves of her red sweater, the way a child might do.

'On the 20th of October 1956, we got engaged,' she says. 'Three days before the revolution.'

She had been twenty-one years old, and living in Budafok. Their two families gathered that Saturday to celebrate the engagement.

The following Tuesday afternoon, Suzanne was at her desk at the railway offices in Pest, where she worked as a clerk. She was looking forward to the end of the day. László had arranged to meet her in a coffee bar, and then they planned to head for home together.

Suzanne's job paid reasonably well, but she hated all the workplace rules. She wasn't allowed to use lipstick or nail polish, and couldn't wear fashionable clothes or shoes.

'You can't grow up in the normal way, you can't be a woman in the normal way, because they tell you how to comb your hair!'

It seems trivial to me at first, to be worrying about your hair. There were much worse abuses imposed by the régime. But then I think her remarks might go to the heart of it, could help explain why hatred of the system ran so deep. It was the State's intrusion into the smallest and most personal freedoms that interfered most with everyday life. Suzanne's resentment suddenly makes sense.

László Budaházy had been working that morning at the motor works pump station in Csepel, a large island in the Danube just south of Budapest. He was studying as well, and in the afternoon he caught the train to the city for his classes. But when he and his friends arrived at the technical college, the caretaker informed them there would be no school that day. The caretaker addressed them as 'Sir'. Budaházy picked up on it immediately.

'How come we are 'Sirs' now,' he asked, 'when we were 'Comrades' yesterday?'

'Oh, I don't know,' the caretaker said. 'Just ... something is happening. The students are demonstrating.'

It was around three in the afternoon. Budaházy turned to his classmates. 'Well, there is no school – might as well go and see what this demonstration is all about.'

They set off for the statue of the poet Sándor Petőfi, which stood in a small square by the Danube, not far from the college. They found a large crowd already gathered there. Petőfi's left hand clutched a scroll, and his right arm was upraised as if addressing the students below. Someone from the crowd had climbed up on the plinth, and was reciting Petőfi's poem: 'Arise, Hungarians!'

Soon afterwards, some of the demonstrators began moving off, heading for the Stalin statue. Budaházy and his friends decided to join them. But the afternoon was slipping away. As they reached Sztálin Square, Budaházy suddenly remembered that he had arranged to meet Suzanne. She would be waiting for him at the coffee bar, unaware of what was happening.

Leaving his friends at the square, he caught a tram to the coffee bar. Suzanne was there. He told her about his strange afternoon, and she became as excited as him. Nothing like this had ever happened before, as far as they could remember. Not wanting to miss any of it, they rushed back to the Stalin statue together.

By the time they arrived, the square was completely filled. Budaházy and Suzanne squeezed in beside one of the streetlamps.

'I lifted Suzi up so she could see better. And the workers in Csepel brought some oxy-acetylene torches, because in the semi darkness we saw the light – the blue light of the acetylene cutting torch.'

Around them, everyone was yelling: 'Cut the bastard! Cut him down!'

The men with the torches managed to sever one of Stalin's legs. Strong steel rods protruded from the inside. They began pulling on the statue again.

'There was such a quiet when it started to move. You could hear it squeaking, because the metal had to bend first. And it was so quiet, you could feel if somebody had dropped a penny, you could have heard it. We were standing like this …' Budaházy sucks in his breath sharply. 'Didn't even breath! Just watching.'

'It was so quiet, I don't think that anybody was breathing in there,' Suzanne agrees.

The trucks strained at the chains around Stalin's neck. Very slowly, the statue began to tilt.

'Eight thirty-five,' Budaházy says. 'That's when his head hit the concrete. I heard it, and I checked my watch.'

He knew, even then, that he would want to remember forever the precise moment when the dictator was toppled.

Suzanne Budaházy, less comfortable with English than her husband, has so far left most of the storytelling to him. But now her voice tumbles over his.

'Everybody was … ooohhh!'

'Such a yelling that you couldn't imagine! It was absolutely – it's very hard to describe. It was like a relief.'

'You have to have lived in Hungary before this happened. You have to imagine how you feel about that, when you're thinking it's all gonna end. And you can live a normal life! In that moment, you go through everything – your whole life, everything.'

'It's like, something's gonna change now. Something's gonna change – because after that, you either all die, or you get rid of the Communists! Because I knew that the Russians will not let this go – I knew that! When that head hit the concrete, I knew this: there's gonna be something.'

In the square, men were attacking the fallen statue with sledgehammers. The crowd was thinning rapidly. László and Suzanne decided they had seen enough. They managed to find a trolley bus that was still running, and it took them as far as Deák Square, in the centre of Pest. Then they caught a second tram around the körút. They were heading for the suburban station at Móricz Zsigmond körtér, in Buda. From there they could get the train home.

But before they crossed the river, the tram passed the Museum. As it did so, László heard an unmistakable cracking noise. Rifles were being fired. He turned to Suzanne.

'Let's go back to Deák Square.'

His sister lived there – he thought he would drop Suzanne off, and then return to the Museum by himself. He wanted to find out where the rifle shots were coming from.

But Suzanne refused to go along with his plan.

'No way! If I let you go to see, what's gonna happen to me afterwards? I won't know what's going on.'

She wanted to get home to Budafok. Her mother would be waiting for her, and László's mother would be worried as well. She pleaded with László to take her home.

'And we just got engaged three days before,' Budaházy points out. 'So I said: All right, all right!'

From Móricz Zsigmond körtér in Pest, they caught the last train back to Budafok. It was after midnight by the time they arrived. László went home and tried to get some sleep. But at three in the morning a deafening rumble woke him. His family lived directly over the main southwestern artery into Budapest. The sound was coming from the road below. Budaházy jumped out of bed and went to the window.

'I looked out, and I saw the tanks and trucks full of Russians coming – a huge number. Couldn't count them.'

His instinct had been right – the Russians were not about to let this go.

The following morning, László and Suzanne met up with their friends. The young people of Budafok had always formed a close-knit group. Most of the boys had managed to avoid their

96

compulsory military service – some had arranged false medical certificates, others were in sports teams and exempt. Budaházy himself had worked as a ship engineer, travelling the Danube from the Black Sea to the Black Forest, and had never stayed in one place long enough for the authorities to find him.

Before the War, some of their fathers had established a rowing club on the Danube, holding regattas in the heat of summer. Their children used to gather at the clubhouse. In the early 1950s, the Communists took the clubhouse away. But that didn't stop the young people from meeting.

They moved to a local coffee bar instead, adopting it as their own. And when the weather was good, they gathered upriver from where the clubhouse had been, on a sliver of gravel beach beneath a grassy slope. It was here that László first met Suzanne, when she was just sixteen years old.

'That's why the Communists hated us,' Budaházy explains. 'They called us the Golden Youth of Budafok.'

The police would regularly come into the coffee bar and demand to see everyone's identity cards. They wanted to know how the boys could afford to buy a cup of coffee. Budaházy was taken to the station on the main square a few times, where he was forced to prove that he had a job – it was illegal not to work. On one of these occasions, police lieutenant Ersai gave Budaházy a beating.

As the lieutenant was hitting him, Budaházy said: 'You are big heroes here, do what you want to me. But if I see you on the riverbank I will kill you, I tell you now.'

Budaházy hadn't dreamed that his chance for revenge was about to come, much sooner than he thought.

Softly-spoken István Pálos was also one of the Budafok group. But on the morning following the Russians' arrival he had not yet returned from the city. He was wandering the streets of Pest, hungry and exhausted, about to visit his cousins.

Also missing that day was Vilmos Schmidt, a truck driver who was a favourite with the younger boys of the district. Schmidt used to take the boys camping, teach them how to cook the *bogrács* on the fire, and how to fish with their hands. Vili was also stuck in Pest, fighting with the insurgents at the Kilián Barracks on Üllői út.

The members of the 'Golden Youth' who were in Budafok that Wednesday morning quickly agreed they should try to find out what was happening. The trains were no longer running, and so they started walking the eight kilometres into the city. Suzanne wanted to return to the railway office where she worked. She had left a pair of glasses and other personal things in her desk drawer, and she wanted to pick them up. But they only managed to get as far as the Gellért hotel in Buda, beside the Szabadság bridge. From there, they could see that every bridge across the Danube was blocked by Russian tanks.

'We stood on the Gellért side and we looked right into the barrels of the tanks.'

Suzanne's workplace was just across the river, but it was clear that there was no hope of reaching it. The sight of the tanks unnerved her.

'Let's go,' she said. 'I don't like this.'

László was holding her hand, and he felt her begin to tremble. They walked back along the embankment to the Móricz Zsigmond körtér, where they stayed for a while, uncertain what to do next. There were large numbers of people milling about in the square. Along one side of the square, a line of women was queuing for bread and milk.

The weather was cool, and at that time of year the nights drew in early. By late afternoon most of their group was ready to head back to Budafok. The sound of gunfire floated across from Pest, but with all the bridges blocked they realised there was nothing more that they could do. They started to drift towards home. Only one young man – Öcsi Schäffer – decided to stay on a little longer.

László and Suzanne were almost home when a man on a bicycle caught up with them. He told them that a Russian tank had fired into the crowd at Móricz Zsigmond körtér. The shell had landed in the middle of the busy square. Shrapnel had scattered everywhere.

The cyclist said: 'There was one kid from Budafok who got hit.'

Budaházy immediately thought of Öcsi Schäffer.

But it wasn't until a few days later, when the revolution seemed to be succeeding, that they heard what had happened to their friend. Budaházy and a few others commandeered a jeep, and they drove over to see Öcsi's mother. The boy's body had been taken there. A piece of shrapnel had hit him in the throat. It had struck with such force that it had taken off the back of his head.

Budaházy and his friends picked up the body and placed it in the jeep.

'When we lifted him up, you could see from the back to his eyes – the light came through his eyes. There was nothing in it, the whole thing was gone.'

The men drove around Budafok, with Öcsi's body on display.

'We told them: "This is what the Communists did to us – let's do something about it!"'

It was all the prompting anyone needed. The organisation of Budafok's resistance, the gathering together of men and weapons, began.

ON THE SECTION of the wide, curving boulevard – the körút – that runs close to the Radio studios stands a grand, white Neoclassical building. This is the Hungarian National Museum, nestled among well-tended gardens. At the main entrance, which overlooks the körút, a set of wide stone steps leads up to a colonnade of eight fluted columns under a triangular portico. It was from these steps that, one spring day in 1848, the poet Sándor Petőfi declaimed his poem: 'Arise, Hungarians! Shall we be slaves, or shall we be free?'

The rear of the Museum faces a narrow backstreet. On the far side of the street is the Radio complex, several buildings clustered around a white-railed courtyard.

In the autumn of 1956, Sándor Tóth had become very familiar with the winding narrow paths and intimate clearings of the Museum gardens. It was a popular place with courting lovers, and in the weeks before the uprising he had been there several times with his girlfriend and another couple.

On the evening of 23 October, the truck that brought Tóth and his friend István from the toppled Stalin statue deposited them in front of the Museum. The crowds already packing Bródy Sándor utca, but Tóth knew exactly where to go. He knew how to get up close to the Radio.

In his chaotic Melbourne living room, Sándor Tóth is possessed by his story, waving away the mugs of coffee offered by his wife, ignoring the cakes she brings out for us. He pushes relentlessly on, the words tumbling fast, never pausing, chasing the memories that stay always just ahead. The hours are passing, but he seems driven to complete his story tonight, however long it takes.

Tóth and István arrived at the boulevard to find trams overturned on the road, their windows smashed. The steel tramlines had been ripped from the ground. There were people everywhere, running through the Museum gardens, and jammed into the surrounding side streets. Realising they couldn't get down Bródy Sándor utca because of the crowds, he and István went into the gardens instead. They headed straight for the back of the Museum.

The gardens were enclosed at the rear by a wrought iron fence, higher than street level. It was a four-foot drop from the foot of the railings to the pavement.

The two young men pushed themselves right to the front, up against the railings. There they had a clear view across the street towards the Radio buildings. The Kossuth Studio was on the left, at the corner with Bródy Sándor utca; to the right was the Petőfi Studio. A courtyard lay between the two studios, sealed off by wrought iron fencing.

The courtyard was filled with ÁVO men. Tóth estimated there must have been over a hundred of them. They were armed with machine guns. Eying the crowd through the railings, the ÁVO men directed uncertain glances at one another.

The largest concentration of demonstrators was at the main entrance, around the corner in Bródy Sándor utca. It was about fifty metres from Tóth. They were demanding to be let in, to have their sixteen points read out over the air. The Security Police were holding them back.

All of a sudden, from that direction, the clear sound of shots rang out.

'It was a shock to me,' Tóth says. 'I didn't expect that to happen.'

The shots were followed by screams, close to the Radio's entrance. There were shouts of terror and impotent anger. People tried to escape the area, but the narrow streets were too crowded, leading to total confusion. Then the ÁVO men in the courtyard opposite Tóth opened fire. They aimed their machine guns directly into the panicking crowd.

Tóth is surprisingly calm as he recalls that night. His voice is level, matter-of-fact, as he tells me that the Security Police were using mostly harmless blanks.

'When they opened up, the whole Museum gardens was loaded, jam-packed with people. If they were really using live rounds, there would have been thousands of people dead within minutes. Probably out of every one hundred bullets, there was one live bullet. And of course, people died – I don't know how many, maybe two hundred people died as a result – but this would have been a bloodbath if they really opened up.'

Tóth has said before that he doesn't like to read books about the uprising – they trigger bad memories for him, as well as feelings of guilt and regret. Like everyone else I have spoken to, he insists from the start that he was not a hero, he was simply there, and played only a small part. In Tóth's case, the statement is tinged with wistfulness, as over an opportunity not completely grasped. As if it had been his finest hour, and he had failed to fully live it.

But we have not yet reached the parts of the story that are most difficult for him – for the moment, the events are still an adventure, exciting for the young man he was then. Tóth is eager, enthusiastic, as he tells me what happened next.

When the ÁVO began firing into the crowd, Tóth knew exactly what to do. As a teenager, he had learnt the techniques of freedom fighting, under the leadership of Communist army officers. He had been shown how to use a rifle, how to take over an enemy position, and how to crawl.

When the firing started, Tóth and István immediately hit the ground. Bullets whistled over their heads. People ran past them, trying to get away. The two friends kept low, crawling back through the gardens with their bellies to the earth. Until finally, protected by the bulk of the Museum building, they could stand and get back onto the main boulevard. From there, they headed towards nearby Kálvin Square.

They found a large crowd gathered there as well. People were shouting about getting weapons, arming themselves somehow, so that they could go back to the Radio and fight. A number of trucks were standing around the square, their engines idling. They started pulling out one by one, heading off along Üllői út in search of weapons.

Tóth jumped up on one of the trucks and rode it out to his home district of Kőbánya, where there was a large munitions factory. When they arrived, the gates were locked shut. The security men on duty that night were determined to stick to their orders. Although terrified, they refused to open up to the mob. But the leading trucks in the convoy had already got hold of weapons from somewhere else.

'You bloody well open it now, or you'll get one yourself!' one of the insurgents cried, pointing his gun at the security men. 'Get the key for the storehouses!'

The men on the gate backed down.

Inside the storehouses, the insurgents found what they were looking for. There was row upon row of military rifles, thousands of guns. Tóth picked out a bolt-action rifle for himself. Then everyone climbed back on the trucks. Zigzagging wildly along Üllői út, they headed into town.

By the time they returned, the streetlights had all been shot out. Kálvin Square and the streets around the Museum were blanketed in darkness. The relentless sound of gunfire signalled the intensity of the fighting. Insurgents who had managed to find guns had already taken up positions in the Museum gardens. They were firing at the ÁVO men in the Radio buildings opposite. There were no more blanks now – on both sides, the ammunition was live.

Somewhere along the way, Tóth and István had lost contact with each other. Alone and clutching his rifle, Tóth thought he would try to get into the gardens and join the fighting there. He could see the wrought iron fence of the gardens a few yards away. But there was a street running alongside the Museum that he needed to cross first. The ÁVO were using tracer bullets that shone in the dark, leaving an imprint of their path. The street was a lacework of speeding lines of light.

Close by Tóth was a Hungarian Army officer who had taken the side of the insurgents. He was giving out orders to anyone who would listen.

'All right, fellows – in one line! We're going to run one after the other into the yard, next to the fence.'

Tóth stared at the officer in disbelief. Turning back, he watched the ÁVO bullets flying along the street. He felt paralysed by fear, and realised he couldn't go through with it. The men around Tóth noted his small frame, his hesitation.

'All right, Mister,' one of them said. 'If you won't go ...'

And he snatched Tóth's rifle away from him.

Settled comfortably on his sofa, Tóth gazes across the room. He stares down the dark tunnel of the past at a young man stripped of his weapon and his dignity. We have arrived at one of the still-sharp points of his regret.

'So in a way I felt a bit ashamed. A coward, and all that. But I could hear the screaming and the yelling in the dark, of people inside who had been suffering, who had been shot. And a lot of people died after that.'

That night, Tóth would be given a second chance to face his fears, and become the person he desired to be. But first, he had to find another weapon. Unable to get any closer to the Museum, he returned to Kálvin tér, where the trucks were about to head out again. Jumping up quickly, he rode to the Kilián Army barracks, a short distance away on Üllői út.

In the barracks storehouse, he found a long line of rifles, shining in their racks. Among them was a German Mauser, in excellent condition.

'Oh, you'll be mine!' he whispered, as he took the rifle down. 'I'm not gonna let *you* go, for sure!'

He returned to the Museum and made his way back to the side street. Another Army officer had taken the place of the first, and a group of insurgents had gathered around him. It was the same routine – run across the street, towards the shelter of the gardens. What was different was that the new officer came from an infantry division. The infantry had a long-held, deep hatred for the Security Police, and the officer didn't hesitate. He plunged straight into the hail of bullets, leading by example. One by one, the other men followed.

Tóth watched them run out onto the exposed street, the phosphorous lines of the tracer bullets carving up the air around them. His thoughts were a confusion of fear and a sense of duty.

'Bugger it,' he decided at last. 'Whatever will happen, will happen.'

Tóth launched himself after the others, racing across the road, forcing his mind clear and focusing only on the wall that was his destination. Reaching it, he slid down the stone. The bullets had missed him, he was safe. But he couldn't stay where he was. On all fours like a dog, he crawled rapidly along the wall, following it around the gardens while all the time keeping in close against the brick, until the Museum was directly between him and the Radio, and he was out of the line of fire. Tóth crawled through a gateway in the wall. He was in the gardens again.

Moving quickly, he headed for the rear of the Museum. It was in complete darkness. He could barely see to put one foot in front of another, but he could hear well enough. Groans and muted screams rose to greet him. The wounded and the dying lay all around, among the planted beds. There was nothing he could do to help them, he knew – it would take everything he had just to look out for himself. He was almost glad that he couldn't see. The stuttering of machine guns came from directly ahead. His legs kept carrying him towards it.

Now he could see the ÁVO's guns, flashing in the night. They were less than a hundred metres away, through the railings. Tóth glanced around. There was a small statue nearby that he thought he could use for cover. Hunching down beside the pale stone, he readied his weapon, took a deep breath, then lunged out from behind the statue. Firing off a shot, he ducked back.

Over and over again Tóth fired his Mauser, not seeing anyone in the darkness, not aiming at anything specific, only firing wildly towards the Radio building and hoping that some of the shots would find their mark. He lost all sense of time. There was only the noise, the blackness, the rapid flaring of the ÁVO's guns ahead, the rhythm of reloading, firing, ducking back, in the autumnal gardens where he had strolled with his girlfriend – when? It seemed so long ago. How had it come to this?

Suddenly there was a shout behind him. Tóth spun around. It was a boy, about fifteen years old. The boy crawled up close to Tóth, raised his gun, and steadied the barrel on Tóth's shoulder to take aim. Before Tóth could stop him, the boy had pulled the trigger. The gun exploded beside Tóth's right ear. After the shock, there was only deep silence on that side. The flesh of Tóth's ear burned fiercely. He wanted to leap up and strike the boy with the butt of his rifle, but above their heads bullets continued to whizz through the trees. He forced himself to stay down.

Over the next hour, Tóth's hearing gradually returned, like rising slowly through water. The stinging sensation died away. Time wore on. The fighting around him was as fierce as ever, a nightmare he could not wake from. Then Tóth heard a deep rumbling, like thunder. The sound cut through the clatter of firing, and seemed to be coming from the side street that Tóth had dashed across earlier. There were shouts, voices raised.

Suddenly, there was a tremendous explosion, which he felt more than heard. The ground shook with the force of it. Tóth flattened himself into the earth, shielding his head with his hands. The blast was followed by an eerie silence. The chatter of guns had stopped.

When Tóth dared to raise his head, he was astonished at what he saw. The large, dark bulk of a tank rose up a bare few metres from him. Somehow, as the tank had come rolling through the gardens, its caterpillar tracks had managed to miss his body. A second tank was standing in the side street. Both belonged to the Hungarian Army, and their cannons were aimed directly at the Radio buildings. From the area where the first shell had hit, no more firing came. The ÁVO continued to shoot from undamaged sections of the building, but things were much quieter than before.

The arrival of the tanks had got everyone excited: the Hungarian Army was on their side! There was a new sense of urgency. The insurgents were keen to press their advantage.

'We can't storm the Radio from this side,' Tóth heard a man close to him say. 'But around the back they're renovating the place.'

Because of the renovations, he thought the rear of the buildings might not be so well protected. He, Tóth and several others decided it was worth a try. They left the Museum gardens, emerging onto the körút and circling around. A narrow backstreet led them straight to the rear corner of the Kossuth Radio building.

Scaffolding covered the studio walls. On the ground, a fire was burning. A group of insurgents was already in place – they had built a barricade out of cobblestones torn from the road, and pieces of other debris. With Tóth's group, they numbered around a hundred altogether. Using the barricade for cover, the insurgents fired past the scaffolding. The ÁVO shot back.

Tóth was taking aim with his rifle when the young man beside him suddenly went down. The ÁVO were using dumdum bullets – bullets with an exposed lead nose that caused them to mushroom open on impact, rather than pass cleanly through the body. They were designed to cause maximum damage to organs and soft tissue. One of these bullets had slammed into the young man's chest. Blood trickled from his mouth. He was still alive, but barely.

Tóth dropped his rifle and went to help. He and some of the others lifted the young insurgent off the ground. Tóth thought he looked about twenty years old. They carried him away from the barricade and through the streets. There was a hospital nearby and it didn't take them long to reach it. But they were too late to save the young man.

It was around four in the morning. Tóth was lingering in the hospital corridors when he heard a prolonged rumble from the distance. He knew what it meant – he had been expecting it for some time. His heart sank. If it had just been the ÁVO, they might have stood a chance. But what hope did a handful of freedom fighters have against the power of the Red Army's tanks? He had just watched a man die. It was a reminder that none of them was immune, that the next bullet might easily be for him.

He had dropped his precious Mauser back at the Radio building. It would certainly have been picked up by now, another insurgent's lucky find. Even so, Tóth decided to return to the barricades. There was nothing for him to do at the hospital, after all.

He found the fighting still continuing, under a sky that carried the first faint traces of dawn. Tóth stood about in the cold, grey morning, and in the camaraderie of battle he struck up a conversation with a Jewish man. Their talk was interrupted when two Soviet armoured vehicles turned suddenly into the street.

The machine guns mounted on the vehicles' roofs began sputtering wildly. Bullets rattled out in all directions, a deadly confetti. The insurgents scattered, scrambling for cover. Tóth noticed a large wooden sand box further along the street – tram drivers used the sand for their brakes. He raced towards the box, cursing his short legs. He had never been good at running. He dived behind the sandbox just as a volley of bullets flew over his head and smacked into the wall behind, raining plaster down on him.

At first, all Tóth felt was relief that he was safe. Then he suddenly realised that his Jewish friend was no longer with him. He looked up and saw the man lying in the street. A shot in the chest had killed his new friend outright.

The Russians had arrived too late to hold the Radio, however. By eight that morning, the ÁVO defending it had run out of ammunition. The insurgents stormed the building, and walked along the corridors checking rooms one by one. Civilian staff members, who had been trapped inside all night, were released. Surviving ÁVO men were either killed or captured. It was an important victory for the freedom fighters, and helped to fuel their confidence.

But the struggle was no longer about the Radio, if it ever had been. The battle had grown much broader than that.

Tóth had not slept all night, but still he was not ready to return home. He made his way instead to the Corvin cinema, across the road from the Kilián Barracks. There, a large group of mostly young insurgents had been battling the Soviet tanks.

The cinema lay just behind the main road, at the corner of the Nagykörút and Üllői út. Snipers had taken up positions in the surrounding apartments. Using a petrol pump at the rear of the cinema, the insurgents stockpiled Molotov cocktails. The iconic weapon of the streetfighter was made by pouring petrol into empty bottles, stoppering them, and tying scraps of rag around the bottlenecks. As soon as the rag was set alight, the bottle was ready to be hurled at its target. They were especially effective against the tanks.

When Tóth arrived at the Corvin it was fully light, and the fighting was tailing off. An anti-tank gun captured from the Russians had been set up on the front steps of the cinema. None of the younger insurgents knew how to use it. An older man among them, Falábú Jancsi – wooden-leg John – had taken control. Falábú Jancsi was an experienced soldier who had lost his left leg in the War. He struck a gruff, forbidding figure in his uniform, with a round of rifle ammunition slung diagonally across his chest, and his left trouser leg rolled up above his wooden peg. Around his neck hung a pair of binoculars, which he used to set the aim of the anti-tank gun.

Falábú Jancsi had positioned the gun so that it stared down the Nagykörút towards the Petőfi Bridge. As the Russian tanks crossed the bridge, Jancsi fired at their chains to disable them. Several of the young freedom fighters were working with him at the anti-tank gun, helping to reload and position it. Tóth would have liked to join them, but Jancsi chased him away.

He went across to the school in Prater utca instead. The insurgents were using it as a base for the wounded, taking care of people there until they could be moved to a hospital. But without a weapon, there was little that Tóth could do. The Corvin was not far from the dried noodle factory where Tóth worked, but already that seemed to him like a different world, one that he couldn't imagine ever returning to. Finally, feeling so exhausted that he could barely stand, Tóth left the Corvin and walked quietly home.

THE CORVIN is still a cinema, but now it seems they not only screen films here, they shoot them as well. I arrive in time to see a man in a leather jacket, his dark hair pulled back into a ponytail, leap up onto the railings by the cinema's entrance, and then jump down again. He shouts something, breaks into a run, then pulls up and wanders casually back. After some discussion with a small filming crew, he repeats the sequence again.

A set of broad steps leads up to the cinema doors. A young boy with a mountain bike waits at the top of the stairs, watching the film crew. Behind him, the curving, creamy yellow wall of the Corvin looks freshly painted. Mel Gibson's *The Passion* will be showing soon.

The cinema occupies the centre of a tidy pedestrian area. Six-storey buildings of cool, pale stone sweep grandly around both sides, enfolding the Corvin in a pair of protective arms. The cinema is the golden nugget at the heart of the embrace.

Directly opposite the Corvin's entrance, at the point where the two curving arms almost meet, there is a passageway out onto the Nagykörút – the broad, tree-lined boulevard that sweeps around Pest on the Danube's eastern side, enclosing the city and defining its shape. From the main road, you might never realise the cinema was there, shielded as it is by the tall buildings. Protected, but with good access to the main road, it was the perfect place for the freedom fighters to make their stand.

The film crew has moved on. The boy rides his bike up and down a ramp leading to the cinema doors, turning sharply at each end. Just in front of him stands another young man, about the same height and age. But this boy is a dark metal statue, with a beret on his head, clutching a rifle pointed towards the ground.

Today is a public holiday, and someone has tied a red, white and green ribbon around the statue's neck. Wreaths, fresh flowers and more ribbons adorn his hands, and colour the grey slab of stone at his feet. Someone takes care to keep the memory alive.

I am taking photographs when a man approaches me. He is stick-thin, in early middle age, his fine black hair greased back. He has a small, brown dog with him, on a lead.

I have a Hungarian face. People often come up to me on the street, to ask the time although I don't wear a watch, or wanting directions to places I've never heard of. On the surface it must seem as though I belong, but the language gives me away. As soon as I open my mouth they stare at me, startled, as if seeing me for the first time. Then they usually turn and stalk off, without another word. As if I had been deliberately trying to trick them, pretending to be something I'm not.

But the thin man is not asking for a favour, he is offering one.

'Would you like me to take your picture?' He points to the cinema and smiles.

'Thank you – but no.'

'I promise I won't run away with your camera.'

'I didn't think you would,' I laugh, relieved that my accent hasn't scared him off. I try to imagine the dog's tiny legs pumping as they both make a dash for it, and laugh again. 'It's just that I don't want to have my picture taken.'

The man shrugs. His shoulders are bony under his loose-fitting jacket. He seems keen to stay and talk for a while. I explain that I am interested in the uprising, and that my father left Hungary in 1956.

'The Kádár years were hard.' He shakes his head sadly.

They were the long years of Communism after the revolution, thirty-two of them under the same leader. The life of János Kádár, a fit man who liked to play chess, was marked by a series of betrayals. A few years after the war, he betrayed his former friend and fellow Communist László Rajk into making a false confession. Rajk was executed as a result. Then in 1956, Kádár betrayed the freedom fighters. He slipped away from Imre Nagy's short-lived government, which formed following the initial success of the insurgents. He returned in early November with the Soviet tanks, to head a new, pro-Moscow régime. He betrayed Nagy again by playing a part in his execution, eighteen months after the uprising. Finally, he betrayed the Czechoslovakian people, offering Hungarian support to the Russians when they sent their tanks into Prague, quelling the protests of 1968.

Some Hungarians would call Kádár an opportunist, capable of adapting his position to take advantage of any situation. But Kádár himself believed that his actions, all of his betrayals, were necessary to stay true to the one thing that really mattered. He believed in the cause of socialism until the day he died.

'But things are better now,' the oily-haired man says.

I discover the dog's name is Csípek, and he (or she – Hungarian has no gender) is nine years old. A tall woman, walking her unclipped black poodle around the cinema, strolls over to join us. Her hair is short and blonde, and she has the strong, muscular build of a shot-putter. The poodle is one of the larger kind, and reaches to her hips.

'This is my neighbour,' says the thin man. He explains to her who I am, and why I am here.

'Was your father at the Corvin?' demands the woman.

'No, he was only in the countryside.'

'*Ugyanaz*,' the thin man says – it's all the same.

He picks Csípek up and cradles the little dog in his arms like a baby. After chatting for a while longer, the blonde woman leads her

113

poodle away, continuing their circuit of the cinema. The thin man points to the pale, curving apartment building to our left, indicates a window on the ground floor.

'That's where I live.'

Putting Csípek down gently, he produces a business card from his pocket.

'If you have any thoughts about anything,' he says vaguely, 'please get in touch.'

I try to imagine his life at the Corvin köz, this thin man and Csípek together in his flat, his yearning for human contact. I barely glance at the card, only noting his occupation –leather tanner.

It's much later that I realise we never exchanged names, and I pull out his card. That's when I notice the coincidence. It gives me a jolt, although the name is common enough. I have been having a conversation with Imre Nagy.

The apartment phone rings. I am half-expecting it to be for Dr Horváth again, but it turns out to be a friend, Martin.

'How about dinner tonight?'

We arrange a place and a time.

It is late afternoon, and I am feeling exhausted. My body hasn't adjusted yet to European time. I know that if I give in to the urge to rest, it probably never will. Right now, I don't care. I lie down on the bed.

A persistent buzzing noise cuts through my sleep, pulling my consciousness gradually back into the room. The phone is ringing. It has grown dark while I was sleeping – a streetlight outside the unshuttered windows casts a cold glow over the furniture. The clock shows 8pm. I wait for the phone to cease its harsh, persistent drone. But the sound continues. The tone is deeper, the frequency more irregular than it should be.

At last I realise it is not the phone, but the door.

Reluctantly, I roll off the bed. In the book-lined, windowless room that leads to the hallway, I have left a light on – my tormentors will assume that someone is home. They are not likely to stop ringing until I answer. I pad barefoot over the cool parquet floor. A shadow moves behind the door's frosted glass panels.

Outside on the balcony two men are waiting. One wears overalls; the other is younger, more smartly dressed.

'We're looking for Mr István Horváth,' the smart man says.

'He's not here,' I sigh. I explain the circumstances as well as I can. The men exchange glances.

'We need to change the electricity meter.' The smart man is less confident now, but undeterred. He holds out his clipboard. There is a green form on it, and he points to Mr Horváth's name at the top. The overalled man smiles helpfully, and produces a shiny new meter from his bag to show me.

'We need someone to check the numbers, and sign,' continues the smart man. 'Can you do that?'

'I suppose so.'

The electricity box is outside the flat, on the wall beside the door. I watch the overalled man extract the old meter, and replace it with the new one. The apartment lights go out briefly, then flicker on again.

Across the courtyard, on my floor and the one above, shadows move behind warmly lit windows. In the old days, when apartment blocks were still communities, there were no individual meters. Shared light and heating systems were located in the basement of each block. At some point in October every year, after three cold days in a row, the heating would be switched on. It would stay on, running full blast, until spring. When bills came, they were split between residents based on floor area. The first Budapest apartment I ever stayed in ran on that communal system. Most probably it doesn't any more.

The overalled man is packing up his tools. The smart man has already gone, moving on to another apartment. A question forms in my sleep-fogged brain.

'Why exactly are you doing this?'

I don't really expect an answer. The changing of the meters is like some

Kafka-esque ritual – disturbingly surreal, and ultimately inexplicable. But I am wrong. The overalled man has a reason.

'The meters – guarantee – fifteen years,' he says loudly, stressing each word. He seems to think I am intellectually impaired. This must be what it feels like to be a migrant, I realise, struggling with language. At least I don't have to suffer it every day.

'After that – we exchange – for new one.'

It seems plausible, and I am satisfied. But Martin's girlfriend, Viki, will later offer an alternative explanation. The old meters, she will tell me, were easy to tamper with. The insertion of a coin or other metal object in a certain spot would provide hours of free electricity. Most of the city knew the trick, and took full advantage of it. That's why the meters had to be changed.

By the time the meter man leaves, I am running late for dinner. Although if they hadn't come, I would probably still have been sleeping. Martin is waiting for me at the restaurant bar. Taller than the people around him, he is still in his suit and a smart coat because he has come straight from work. It is past eight-thirty, but this is an early night for him.

Martin is from New Zealand, but he has lived in Budapest for more than ten years. Despite this, he still orders from the waiters in English. The food is Mexican, the quality as good as anywhere else in Europe, and that surprises me. There was a choice of cuisine when I lived here before – Chinese, or Italian – but it used to be difficult to get the right ingredients. The food would end up with the special local flavour of fried lard and paprika. Prawn noodles or pizza, everything tasted the same.

Now it's harder to find authentic Hungarian cuisine. The city restaurants cater for tourists, with overpriced menus and aggressive gypsy violinists. To avoid all that, you have to search out the little basement *vendéglős*, marked by hand painted signs over entrances that are little more than holes in the wall. You have to know where to look.

I was brought up on Hungarian food. My father did most of the cooking at home, and the shopping as well. He still enjoys the markets, likes to search out the best vegetables and haggle over the price. He cooked chicken *paprikás*, goulash soup spiced with fresh chillies, cabbage stuffed with beef and rice and fried potato cakes smothered in salt. My father made his own schnitzels, pounding pork fillets until they were flat. Sometimes I would help, dipping the meat into separate plates of egg, flour and breadcrumbs, until my fingers grew a pale, sticky crust.

My aunt Matild was also a busy cook. She was a stout, thick-limbed woman who wore her dark, oily hair scraped harshly back from her face. I remember her in the steamy kitchen in Horváti, toiling over a wood-fired stove. The kitchen was where she slept as well, up against the wall in the stove-warmed room. Her bed doubled as a seat during the day, and her husband, Illés, could often be found stretched out there in the afternoon, sleeping off his wine-fuelled morning.

Whenever we visited Horváti, Illés would sit at the table with us for lunch and dinner. But he would eat no more than a mouthful of the wonderful meals his wife prepared. His eyes smiling and unfocused, he would wave the food away, and pour out a little more wine instead. He was all bone, covered with wiry muscle, and very little flesh. It wasn't unusual in Hungary, where men started the day with a shot of strong *pálinka* brandy. Even the back of my father's old school report card carried a printed warning to parents:

'do not give alcohol to your children. It can impair their concentration, and may result in serious disease'.

Matild looked forward to our visits, to the arrival of family who would appreciate her cooking. She fried peppers and eggs to make breakfast *lecsó*, peeled potatoes at the rough-surfaced table, boiled chicken and vegetables for *csirke leves*. She was proud of her chicken soup, the quality of it apparent in the colour and clarity of the strained stock. The best stock was translucent, a rich golden yellow, like liquid afternoon sun. The colour reflected onto my aunt's shiny face as she carried the bowl carefully to the table, gripping it with both hands so that it wouldn't spill. Whenever we arrived at the house, there were always *sütemények* – small homemade cakes and fancy biscuits – to welcome us, and there was always a smile on my aunt's round face.

IT WAS EARLY November, 1956. The main road leading into Hungary from the Ukrainian border shuddered under the weight of an endless column of tanks, trucks and armoured cars. The Red Army was on its way to Budapest.

At his barracks in Ligettanya, my father listened to the tanks' metal caterpillar tracks clattering on the concrete road surface. The noise continued for a full day and night, without pause. Soviet helicopters passed over the barracks, their broad blades whistling. They were bringing in equipment to support the troops.

Still no one had come to relieve Péter. Even though, technically, his three years of service were over, if he left now without being formally discharged it would make him an army deserter. And desertion was a crime punishable by execution in front of a firing squad.

Against the background noise of the invading Soviet forces, Péter met with two friends that he trusted.

'We should desert,' one of them said, 'and try to reach home on foot.'

Péter's home in Horváti was roughly seventy kilometres away across open country. His friends Zoltán and Mihály lived in a similar direction, between the Tisza and the Bodrog rivers. The journey would be difficult and dangerous.

They looked at each other, and agreed to give it a try.

At eight o'clock that night, Péter and Zoltán were rostered on guard duty at the base. Mihály slipped out to join them at the sentry box. The three men felt apprehensive, but were keen to be on their way now that the decision had been made.

Because he was on duty, Péter was armed with a submachine gun. He thought the weapon might come in useful during the journey ahead. But carrying a weapon was too much of a risk – it was a greater offence than desertion alone. If he were caught with it, he could be executed on the spot. So Péter took off his gun, and placed it on the floor of the guards' cabin before they left.

The three friends set off on foot for the small town of Baktalórántháza, using the railway tracks as a guide. The noise of the Soviet tanks on the main road increased in intensity, telling them they were drawing closer. The night sky glowed with an unnatural, cool light, and at first they didn't understand it. Then they realised it was cast by the powerful headlamps of the Red Army vehicles.

Baktalórántháza was on the other side of the main road. Beyond the town were the open fields of their route home. There was no way around it – they would have to get across the road somehow.

When they reached it, the men hid among the dark shadows of winter-bare acacia trees. The trees protected them from the beams of the tanks. For the first time, they saw the tanks and armoured trucks for themselves. Up close, the noise was deafening. The earth trembled beneath the long, slow-moving line.

At first, a crossing seemed impossible. Then they noticed that the stream of traffic was not actually continuous. The vehicles were organised into separate companies, which advanced one after the other. Between the units, for a few brief moments, the road was clear.

The men waited. At the next gap they broke from the cover of the trees and raced across the concrete, terrified that the headlamps of the oncoming unit would suddenly reach them, and they would be frozen in the light. But they managed to get safely to the other side.

Passing through Baktalórántháza, they headed across the fields to the next village. Mihály knew a family there who would put them up for the night. The ground was under two inches of snow, and the going was hard. It was late by the time they arrived at the village, and they were glad to get inside. Too on edge to sleep, they sat up in the house until daybreak. Then, before anyone in the village could wake and see them, they set off again.

Throughout the next day they tramped through the fields, keeping roughly to a northeasterly direction. The journey was lengthened and complicated by the need to circle around any villages or towns. Too conspicuous in their army uniforms, they dared not risk showing themselves.

The temperature was close to freezing, but the movement and adrenaline of the journey helped to keep them warm. The military training they had endured on the Puszta – all those nights spent in exercises on the frozen plain – came in useful now. All three of them were country boys, used to unforgiving weather. Still the rough earth, rigid with frost, jolted their legs. The stiff leather of their boots rubbed the skin from their feet.

In the rush of leaving they had not thought to bring food with them, only a little money, and hunger soon set in. They had no water, either. Scooping snow up from the ground, they crunched it in their mouths. In one field, Péter noticed the signs of an old cabbage crop. The vegetables had been picked some time ago, leaving tough stalks behind. The three of them dropped to their knees and gouged the stalks out of the earth with their hands, then swallowed them raw. It was nowhere near enough to fill their stomachs, but it helped take the edge off their hunger.

Night fell. They made a bed for themselves in a haystack and tried to get some sleep, but the cold penetrated their dreams and continually jerked them awake.

The following morning was more of the same – bitter weather, frozen ground jarring their bones, sore feet. Their gnawing hunger

121

was starting to sap their strength. Then, around noon that day, they reached the Tisza River.

The Tisza, broad and long, follows the northern edge of the Great Plain for several kilometres before turning south towards Szeged. It slices the Plain in two on its downward sweep. The landmark gave the three men their bearings – Mihály and Zoltán were close to home. Even Péter, who had the furthest to travel, was more than halfway. They began to dream of soft beds, warm firesides and full bellies, the faces of family and friends.

But first, they had to cross the Tisza. They had expected to find it frozen over, the ice firm enough to take their weight. Then it would have been easy – they could simply have walked to the opposite bank. But instead, to their dismay, they found the Tisza flowing strongly. The current was fierce and the water numbingly cold. They would never be able to swim it.

There was nothing to do except keep walking, along the bank of the wintry river, following its course downstream. They hoped for a bridge. Péter also scanned the ground for materials that might be used for a makeshift bridge of their own.

There was nothing. But what they found, before they had been walking for very long, was a fisherman, out alone on the water.

'Will you help us get across the river?' Péter asked. 'We can pay you.'

The fisherman took their money and ferried them to the opposite bank in his boat. He would have noticed their uniforms, but he asked no questions. By that time, word of the uprising had reached even the remoter parts of the country. The fighting had spread beyond Budapest, to places like Debrecen, Szeged and Miskolc. In the western town of Mosonmagyaróvár, eighty-eight unarmed demonstrators had been gunned down by the Security Police. Everything was in suspension, none of the old rules applied.

Once they were safely on the northern bank of the Tisza, Mihály peeled off to the left, heading for his village. Péter and Zoltán

122

continued straight on together, towards Semjén on the Slovak border, where Zoltán's family lived.

The sky was turning dark by the time they arrived. Zoltán's parents were astonished but delighted to have their eldest son returned to them, out of the blue.

'Wait here. I'll heat some water on the stove for you,' Zoltán's mother said.

The boys washed away the filth of their journey. When they were clean, they found the table piled high with food. They ate until their stomachs could hold no more. Later that night, when Péter pulled off his boots, he discovered that his feet were a mass of blisters. But for the moment at least, he didn't care. He was about to enjoy his first undisturbed night of sleep in three days.

In the morning, Péter awoke feeling rested and refreshed. He dressed, intending to start out on the final leg of his journey. But when he tried to pull his boots on, he winced with pain. The stiff leather scraped against his blistered skin. It took all his willpower just to get the boots on. The thought of walking anywhere in them was unbearable.

'Rest here a few days more,' Zoltán's father urged. 'Give your feet some time to heal.'

It was tempting. Péter still had a long road ahead of him. But he was desperate to see his family. If he stopped now, he might lose all momentum, and never make it home.

So Péter set out again, his feet complaining with every step. The road out of Semjén was hard and icy. He was hoping to hitch a lift, but no carts passed him all morning. Finally he reached the bridge over the River Bodrog at Sárospatak, and saw the town's castle looming on the opposite bank. His heart lifted. This was familiar territory at last. It gave him the strength to keep going.

By the time Péter entered the neighbouring village of Tolcsva, in the foothills of the Zemplén Ranges, it was raining. Here at last he was able to get a ride on a horse-drawn cart over the final short section of the journey. The cart dropped him beside the cemetery on the outskirts of Horváti, where the graves of his ancestors looked out across the peaceful green hills. Péter followed the edge of the stream that ran below his neighbours' gardens, and turned into the yard of his own house.

As chance would have it, the entire family was gathered inside – parents, grandparents, younger brother Miklós and sister Matild, as well as some guests, friends from the village. They all pressed around him, staring in amazement. The women fussed over him.

'I can't believe it, that you're home at last!' Tears filled his mother's eyes.

There was no television or radio in the village, but news of the uprising had filtered through. Péter told them what he had seen – the Russian forces streaming over the border. For the moment, everything in Horváti was quiet, but Péter was certain that trouble was on its way.

'It'll only be a matter of time before the Russians come here,' he warned. 'Just like they did in the Second World War.'

The village closed in around itself. Péter organised some of his friends into a small guard unit, and every evening at sunset they walked to the outer edge of the houses. From there they had a clear view of anyone trying to approach the village along the single road in. They stood watch throughout the night.

I AM SITTING in the Mexican restaurant with Martin, staring at an enormous plate of food and wondering how I will ever manage to eat it. I am no longer used to such large meals. It was different when I lived in Budapest – then, we would eat out most evenings, trying the new places as they opened.

Restaurants were cheap by western standards in those early days. It was also easier than shopping for food – hoping to find tomatoes when they were out of season, or buying a whole chicken when all you needed was a single breast. Now Martin tells me he often cooks for himself and Viki, and they stay at home to eat.

I don't manage to finish my tortilla, and it seems such a waste. It is late, but Martin offers to show me the new apartment he has bought. Outside on the street he hails a taxi, instructing the driver in English. We head across the Chain Bridge, then angle sharply upwards through dimly lit cobbled streets. Martin's apartment nestles in the Víziváros district, among the narrow alleyways beneath Castle Hill. Old buildings are jammed up tight against each other, giving the district a claustrophobic feel. As a result, Martin's flat comes as a surprise.

The living area is open plan, spacious and light. One long wall consists of a row of tall windows overlooking the Danube. Through them I can see the bridge we have just crossed. Beyond it, the newly restored basilica is golden under floodlights. Further along the embankment stand the illuminated white buttresses of Parliament.

In his modern kitchen of gleaming white surfaces, Martin opens a bottle of wine and pours out two glasses. There are recipe books beside him, pots planted with basil and coriander, long rows of jars with spices, coloured pasta spirals, lentils and beans. All these little luxuries, which in the West we take for granted, would have been unthinkable in Hungary just a decade ago. I feel I need to pinch myself to check that it is real.

'Hungary's changed,' Martin says, smiling at the astonished look on my face. 'You can get anything here now.'

This makes me vaguely uneasy, but I can't immediately work out why.

'In ten years, why haven't you bothered to learn Hungarian?' I ask. 'Why do you still speak English wherever you go?'

Martin shrugs. 'There's no need to learn the language. Everyone speaks English now.'

'But language is integral to a country's culture. Aren't you interested in the literature, theatre or music of the place you've chosen to live in? I can't believe you'd be that arrogant. You're just incredibly lazy!'

I probably go too far. Too late, I realise my frustration has nothing to do with Martin. It's my own failure to absorb language and culture that I am really angry with. And my nostalgia for a place that no longer exists. If it ever did exist, that is, outside my own romantic imagination.

Martin sinks back on his leather sofa, and calmly drinks his chilled wine. If my accusations have affected him, he doesn't show it. The wall of windows stretches behind him with its hypnotic view. The floodlit arches of the Chain Bridge brighten the darkness of late evening.

The window glass forms a seal between us and the city. It presents a romantic picture, while at the same time locking us out from the reality. This apartment is made for people like Martin and me – wealthy foreigners who are just passing through. We can never be anything else, no matter how hard we try.

Outside, the river races black beneath a glitter of reflected light, hinting at the depths that Martin and I have both somehow failed to reach.

It is difficult to look at a familiar city, and forget what you know. Hard to see it naked again, with the layers of memory and received wisdom peeled away. I have tried it with Budapest, but only once.

It was spring, 1994. My last few months of living in Hungary. A warm day, but with a strong wind. I was living in Pest then, not far from the square where Stalin's statue once stood. The square had become a vast car park, loud with the idling engines of tourist buses. Graffiti stenciled on a grey cabling box read: '*Lehet egy más világ*'. A different world is possible.

That day, my friend Ádám Tóth dropped by. I knew Ádám from work – he was a trainee auditor, a job that failed to make full use of his sharp, inventive mind. He was the only one of my Hungarian colleagues who indulged me in my wish to learn the language, who taught me words, jokes and phrases. He persisted even when I was irritable and tired, when others would have made it easy for me, and themselves, by lapsing into English. Several years younger than me, Ádám's slight frame and mobile, elfin face made him seem younger still, no more than a child.

'I have an idea for a game we could play,' he said.

I wanted to know what the game was, but Ádám refused to say more. Eyes dancing, a sly smile on his face, he urged me into his car.

'But where are we going?'

'You'll find out soon enough.'

He drove a pale blue Trabant. The only upholstery was on the seats – the rest was bare metal, alarmingly thin. The gear stick jutted from the dashboard. Where I would normally expect the gearbox to be, there was a hole in the floor. Mesmerised, I watched the surface of the road flashing past beneath us.

It made me think of a black and white photograph in our family album, showing my father standing beside his first car. It was a brand new, two-seater sports car – an Austin Metropolitan 1500cc, golden-yellow and white.

At first, my father had trouble finding work in England, although he had been brought across as a strong, fit young man to work in the Welsh mines. But the unions had other ideas – they feared British jobs would be taken by the new refugees. He did eventually get work as a miner, and learned English while he trained. The pay was not high however, and after a while he joined the Merchant Navy, exchanging the enclosed underground spaces for an open horizon.

When my father returned from the sea, he had saved enough money to buy the Austin. 'At traffic lights, it would just go!' he says. He can still tell me the exact price he paid for it – 750 pounds. There was a second print of the photograph developed; my father sent it home to Horváti, a symbol of all the possibilities his new life held.

The first cars I remember our family owning were Japanese. Like the Austin, my father always bought them new, and left the clear plastic on the upholstery so it wouldn't be spoiled. I used to get travel sickness from the chemical factory smell. By this time, our family was visiting Hungary fairly regularly. Later, once my brother and I were grown up, my father would usually make the trip on his own, catching a coach that groaned with the heavy luggage of other Hungarians like him, making the long trip home.

But in those early days the whole family would go, taking our car on the ferry across the Channel, and driving without stopping through Belgium, Germany and Austria. It was always the height of summer, the car like an oven even with all the windows wound down. My father driving, my mother beside him irritable with the heat, me and my brother arguing in the back. The border guards terrifying with their rifles and their distant, serious manner. The boot loaded up with blue jeans and other luxurious gifts from the West.

It was the 1970s. In Hungary there was a two-year waiting list for a Trabant, and the full price had to be paid in advance. Wherever we parked our car, we would come back to find it surrounded by small boys and teenagers. They would be peering curiously through the windows, checking the make and model, pushing each other to ask shy but eager questions.

Ádám drove his Trabant towards the Danube, then across the Erzsébet Bridge. As we went, he explained the rules of the game. They were deceptively simple. He had brought his camera – we were to take photographs of the city from a popular sightseeing place.

'But not the sort of photographs that a tourist would take.'

There was the challenge. We had to find new ways of looking at Budapest. Our pictures would reveal the real city, hidden beneath the obvious one of bridges, statues and castles.

He parked on the embankment beside Gellért Hill. The dolomite cliff face soared above us, searing white in the sun. A series of stone steps were cut into the hillside, and we climbed them as far as the statue of Saint Gellért, overlooking the city. This was where we would take our photographs.

Catching my breath after the steep ascent, I gazed along the snaking river, from Margit Island in the north to Csepel in the south. Pest spread far beyond it, a picture-postcard view. I was already stuck. How could I see this city any other way?

We took turns with the camera. I focused in on details – wildflowers in the grass, the texture of a worn stone step. Ádám was much better at the game, more creative. He twisted his body, lay on the ground for unusual perspectives. He pointed the lens straight upwards, took wide-angle pictures of the wind-blown sky.

The roll of film was soon finished, but neither of us was ready to go home. It was still early afternoon.

Ádám had a suggestion: 'Why don't we go up to Széchenyi-hegy? We could walk through the park.'

It seemed like a good idea. We were soon speeding towards the outer suburbs of Buda, as fast as the Trabant could manage, western cars streaming easily past us on both sides. The pitch of the engine rose as the car struggled to climb the hills. Within twenty minutes, we were at the lower reaches of Széchenyi-hegy. Beyond the stone gateway at the park's entrance, scrubby grassland stretched away on all sides. Here the wind was stronger – it lashed the branches of the few scattered trees. Even so, the park was busy with people, mostly families, strolling across the grass.

Ádám and I wandered about for a while. Children raced around us, screaming. My hair whipped across my face. I was beginning to feel cold. We turned back towards the car.

As we approached the entrance, Ádám pointed to a grey rock, the size of a melon, lying on the ground near the gateway.

'I think there's something under there,' he said. 'Why don't you take a look?'

I couldn't see anything, but I lifted the rock to make sure. Ádám watched from a distance, his delicate, slender body holding surprisingly firm against the gusting wind. There was a pale sheet of paper beneath the rock, folded into four. I picked it up, opened it out.

It was a poem.

Ten short lines, in Hungarian. The uneven black ink of a typewriter, the 'a' key striking the page slightly lower than the other letters.

The gate opened
And a naked verse
Stood in the gateway.

I read on. The poem had the feel of Haiku. It was simple and atmospheric, an expression of mood rather than story. It described a blue sky, wind blowing through hair, brilliant sunshine. At the bottom was the author's name: Ádám Balázs Tóth. The paper was fresh and clean – it hadn't been under the rock for long.

The pragmatist in me wanted an explanation. Had he waited for me to turn away, then placed the poem while I was distracted? It seemed he wouldn't have had time. Perhaps he had come up to the park earlier in the day, and had planned from the beginning to bring me here. But Ádám, laughing at my bewilderment, refused to tell me how he had done it. The poet in him insisted on keeping it a mystery, keeping the magic of the moment alive.

In blue biro, the words swerving sideways down the edge of the page, he had written: 'For Anna, with love.'

THE FOG lifted, and the autumn sun shone out.
The sky was clear and blue above the Danube and the
 freed city.

This is part of the poem that the gentle-voiced István Pálos composed to mark the fortieth anniversary of the Hungarian Uprising. He is describing the last days of October 1956, when the Russian tanks pulled out of Budapest, seemingly defeated, and the fighting ceased. A new government was formed, with Imre Nagy at its head.

'Everyone was so happy,' Pálos says of those days of calm.

He is back on the edge of my armchair, a cup of coffee cooling beside him. The second instalment of his story is about to begin.

'We won – full stop. Now it's going to be different. There were the broadcasts from Radio Free Europe and the Voice of America. We called them *kacsa*, the duck – you know the duck goes quack, quack, quack. And they promised everything.'

On one of those days, Pálos walked from Budafok into Pest to take a look around. 'Everyone was on the street – it was full like Melbourne on a Saturday afternoon. Sooner or later, people started to sing the Himnusz, the national anthem. Everywhere! I heard it at least a dozen times in half an hour.'

In his poem, Pálos writes that the streets of Budapest became like an enormous church, under the curve of a sky blue, sunlit dome. Freedom fighters wearing machine guns and belts of hand grenades took up the anthem; an elderly man removed his hat and

132

turned his face to the sky, tears streaming from his eyes. Broken shop windows still had all their products out on display, untouched by looters. Suitcases brimming with money lay in the street, collections for the relatives of the dead.

But there was also evidence of the cost of the win. Young fighters had been laid out on the ground where they fell, their identity cards placed open on their chests. Men and women peered at the details on display – the name, a smiling photograph, an occupation – then shook their heads. 'It's not him…' Afraid of finding the one that they were searching for; and just as afraid that they wouldn't.

'You may understand by now why everybody had a very deep hatred of the Security Police,' Pálos says. 'I personally saw that corpse, hanging down from the tree – you probably saw that picture somewhere? And old ladies, or a mother with a small baby in her arms, bent down and spat at the corpse.'

I know immediately the photograph that Pálos is thinking of. Taken by John Sadovy for *Life*, it is an image that burns off the page with the intensity of the hatred it portrays. In stark black and white, it shows the lynched corpse of an ÁVO man hanging by his ankles from a tree. His arms, entangled in the shirt that has been ripped from his body, brush the ground. The pattern of his ribcage shows through the blood on his bare torso, and his battered face is dark.

A young woman has lunged forward from the crowd that presses around the body. The camera catches her at the moment that she spits on the corpse – her face is slightly blurred with the movement of it.

The picture is mostly dark. The light picks out the man's arms in his white shirt, the litter of cigarettes that have been stubbed out on his body, the young woman's tightly stretched skirt. It shows the expressions of the onlookers, shocking in their calmness, the slight smiles of satisfaction.

'It's hard to understand, but that's what happened,' Pálos says. 'Because her father or brother was persecuted by those people, unjustly. And that was the only thing which had been a stain.'

And underneath the optimism, there was a nagging sense of disquiet that refused to go away.

'Somehow we didn't fully believe that it was finished. The feeling – which I still remember – was a sort of nervousness mixed with fright, mixed with joy, mixed with satisfaction; but mixed with plenty of uncertainty. Uncertainty – that was my personal feeling.'

Now Pálos's story begins to overlap with his friend, László Budaházy's. I piece them both together like a jigsaw puzzle, to make a complete whole.

At the end of October, Vilmos Schmidt, the truck driver who used to take the younger boys camping in summer, returned home to Budafok. The fighting had finished in Pest, he wasn't needed there any more.

'Vili was trained to be an air force fighter pilot,' Budaházy explains, as we sit at his lace-covered dining table.

'So he was the only one of us – because none of us were soldiers, we all managed to somehow get out of the army. And Vili came home with his Tommy gun. We were all in the main square of Budafok, and Schmidty came home with a black face and everything dirty as usual. Because he was always dirty, he was a truck driver.'

The district police headquarters overlooked the parklands of the town square. As Vili arrived with his gun, a policeman approached him.

'What are you doing with this weapon?' the policeman asked.

'It's not your business!'

'You have to give it to me.'

'Take it, then – you take it!'

But the Captain of the police force in Budapest had deliberately refused to give any orders on the uprising. In the absence of specific directions, his men were unsure what to do. The policeman looked at Vili, but didn't make any move towards the gun.

Vili, on the other hand, didn't hesitate. 'Well, we'll take yours!' he declared. 'We'll take the whole police station!'

Budaházy rarely smiles. There is a sombre darkness to his character. He seems to hold all the burden and promise of a long history – not just his own, but inherited from his country as well. Yet occasionally, Budaházy's well-defined mouth will tighten and lift, as if he has eaten something sour. This is the closest he gets to a smile. His lips pucker now.

'So that's how we took the police station, and we told every copper to go home! And Vili organised the whole resistance in our town, he became our leader.'

In the basement of the police building, the insurgents discovered a large armoury with hand grenades and machine guns. They organised regular armed street patrols, working in shifts. They knew by now that the Russian tanks had not completely withdrawn – they had simply dropped back, and formed a tight ring around Budapest.

'Well, I didn't just walk off the wallpaper,' Budaházy says. 'We knew – or at least, I knew – that it's not gonna be finished now. The Russians were waiting for reinforcements. And the railway telegraph told us there are thousands of armour coming through the eastern borders! And the government denied it! Imre Nagy still trusted his stupid Communist Party, he still trusted that they gonna see his view.'

Budaházy knew better, but the lack of military experience among the Budafok group worried him. If the Russians came back, they would be in serious trouble. He approached a good friend of his, who had once been a captain in the Army, for help. But the man refused to get involved.

'I know this, what you've started, is a heroic thing,' the Army captain said. 'I take my hat off for you. But I don't risk my family, my children's future, on a futile thing.'

Did Budaházy also think this way?

'I knew it,' he tells me calmly. 'I knew it was futile.'

Yet he was determined to fight on.

'For eight hundred years, my family was always involved in every war we ever had. Every uprising. Rákoczi, Tököly – every time there was something to do, Budaházys were in it.'

The Budaházy coat of arms is mounted behind the dining table, on the wall beside his kitchen. It shows a soldier clutching a blood-soaked dagger.

'My father did it, my grandfather did it, my uncle did it, my brother did it. Every generation has to do it. And that's why I did it.'

On Sunday 4 November, István Pálos's father woke him before dawn.

'Imre Nagy is on the Radio.'

Pálos rushed to their wireless set. Nagy was announcing that Soviet troops were attacking Budapest. Everyone's worst fears had finally come true.

'Our troops are resisting,' Nagy declared. 'The Government is in its place.' The message was repeated in several languages. It was followed by a plea from the Writers' Union to the rest of the world.

'Help! Help! Help!'

The announcement ended abruptly, and the Radio went off the air, the sudden silence more chilling than the broadcasts themselves.

Pálos dressed quickly. He went down to the insurgents' usual meeting place, at the square in front of the Town Hall. Everyone was there, around thirty men in all.

'We were very determined to do something now, because we had so many promises –from America, from everywhere – and we said: Well, they must help Hungary. They must help.'

The Radio had said that the Russian troops were heading for the centre of Budapest. Budafok lay on the main route into the city from the south, and the freedom fighters' first thought was to try and hold up the Russians at the outer edge of the district. They had two field guns, taken from a local army barracks, and their machine pistols; but nothing else. Nothing that would stop a column of Russian tanks for very long.

'I was sure I gonna die,' László Budaházy says. He, too, had rushed to the town square early that morning, ready to do whatever was necessary. Prepared, even, to die.

Vili Schmidt addressed the group. 'Whoever decides it's too dangerous – go home. And whoever comes – let's go!'

They rode on trucks out to the match factory at Budafok's southern edge, and took up position behind a concrete wall. Budaházy's younger brother had come along too. He was seventeen years old, and Budaházy tried to push him away. He had to strike the boy to make him leave.

'Go home!' he told his brother. 'One dead is enough – go home and look after the family!'

Budaházy knew the thin concrete wall would not withstand the onslaught of a tank's cannon. He was convinced that none of them would survive the day.

'We were waiting for the Russian tanks,' Pálos says. 'But they never came!'

A folding map of Budapest is spread out on my living room floor. Pálos kneels over it, indicates the sprawling lilac patch south of the city that is Budafok. The Danube flows along its eastern edge and past the town square, where the surrounding streets are tiny and dense. Further out, the roads wind and spread, climbing limestone hills.

'Somehow, the Russian column came into here…'

He points to the western edge of the district, to the Balatoni út, a large road that winds up into the hills above the city. The freedom fighters had been waiting over in the east, on the route that leads beside the river directly to the city centre. The Russians had gone a different way, and missed them completely.

'We were lucky,' Pálos says, in his understated way.

When they realised that the Russians had bypassed their blockade, Budaházy and several of the others decided to move the field guns up to the Balatoni út. On the high side of Budafok, the road curved in a sharp S-bend. From that point, there was a magnificent view north, with the whole of Buda stretched out below. They had the idea of setting their guns up on the corner, from where they could shell the Russian positions in the hills.

But first the heavy guns had to be hauled through the district, along steep, narrow streets. It was hard, physical work. At around eleven o'clock at night, Budaházy and his friends were dragging one of the guns up an incline, when they came to a fork in the road.

'We were very tired. We were cold and hungry. And we said, Oh, let's leave this cannon here.'

As Budaházy and his friends stood around the gun, debating what to do, a man emerged from a nearby house.

'What are you doing?' the man asked.

A truck driver called Joe, a young man with a large nose who was always sniffing, answered for the group.

'*Fater*,' Joe said, using the slang form of address for an older man; '*Fater*, have you ever been a soldier?'

'Yes, I've been a soldier!'

'Well, here is this Tommy gun.' Joe handed over his weapon. 'Look after our field gun for us – we'll come back in the morning and pick it up!'

Budaházy chuckles at the memory. 'Mind you,' he says, 'If the Russians came that way and they saw that gun, they would have shot his head to smithereens!'

But the elderly man didn't hesitate. 'All right,' he said. 'I'll look after it, boys – you go home and sleep.'

And he took the Tommy gun and sat with it on the back of the field cannon. When the boys returned the following morning he was still perched there, faithfully guarding the cannon as he had promised to do.

'See, the country was all one,' Budaházy says wistfully. 'It was all one.'

The Russians had set up their heavy artillery in the Buda hills, and were shelling the centre of Pest, across the river. The Budafok insurgents hauled one of their field guns and a wide-barelled machine gun up to the S-bend on the Balatoni út. On the lower side of the road, the ground dropped steeply away into the valley. The insurgents aimed their weapons out across the valley, towards the Russian positions.

On their first night at the bend, while they were still setting up their weapons and hadn't yet fired a shot, a Russian column with three tanks came along the Balatoni út. They were heading for the city. Budaházy heard them approach.

'You don't know what it feels like to hear a tank coming. A 74-ton monster, and big diesel in it and chains rattling. It's terrifying, I tell you! It's absolutely terrifying.'

The single carriageway road ran through a slight cutting. Passing vehicles could be ambushed from both sides without the attackers being seen. Budaházy was hiding by the side of the road with Vili Schmidt, hand grenades and bottles of petrol beside him, ready to throw them at the tanks. Frightened and anxious, eager to get it over with as quickly as possible, Budaházy was about to attack the first tank in the column. But Vili Schmidt had already gone up against the Russians during the earlier fighting in Pest. He knew how it was done.

'Not yet, not yet,' he urged the impatient Budaházy. 'Not yet.'

Budaházy fought down his fear. Two of the tanks rumbled slowly past.

'You always take the last tank,' Budaházy explains now. He takes his cup and a salt pot, and arranges them on the lace-patterned tablecloth to demonstrate. 'If I try to knock this front one out, the tank behind him sees me. So you always try to hit the back one. They can't turn around.'

The third tank in the column trundled towards him. The deafening drone of the chains filled Budaházy's ears. At last he could make his move. Stomach churning, legs trembling, he jumped up and hurled a bottle at the tank. The glass smashed when it hit, and the petrol spread across the metal. Budaházy followed it up with a hand grenade. The grenade exploded, igniting the petrol. The entire tank went up in flames.

It was exactly what Budaházy had hoped for. But, even in that moment of euphoria, there was something darker beneath his happiness, already undermining it. He couldn't forget that there were men trapped inside the burning tank.

'It's difficult to kill somebody,' Budaházy says quietly. 'You feel like puking. And you don't feel very heroic, but you have to live with it. Nobody absolved me from killing a human being. And I am a religious man; and I have to live with it.'

The following morning, István Pálos joined the Budafok fighters at the road bend. Through binoculars, they could see the Russian gun positions across the valley in the Buda hills. They gathered around the long-range field gun, but no one was quite sure how to set it up.

One man had trained with the army as a forward observer. Although he had never used that particular type of cannon, he knew a little about guns. With his help, they tried to work it out.

The cannon came with a sighting instrument, like V-shaped double binoculars. The ex-soldier fastened this to a telegraph pole. Then he demonstrated how to position the shell, and stuff bags of gunpowder in the barrel. A two-metre length of string worked the firing mechanism, igniting the gunpowder and propelling the shell out of the barrel.

The aiming of the gun was more complicated. It was not a case of simply pointing the barrel at the target, because the trajectory of the shell was not a straight line. The shot would fly up at first, then fall back down in a parabolic curve. The gun needed to be set to the co-ordinates of the target, and these had to be calculated with the sighting instrument.

Half the day had disappeared by the time they were ready to fire the first shot.

Pálos makes wide gestures with his hands as he describes the excitement of that initial attempt.

'Ready – fire! Absolutely big smoke. Bang! Whoooosh! Propelled towards Buda.'

One of the fighters had binoculars. He peered eagerly out across the valley, searching for the explosion. Everyone waited. The man shook his head.

'Absolutely nothing! Couldn't see anything!'

They checked the entire arrangement again – the aim, the process for loading the gun. And realised that the shell had not been armed. Because of that, the shell had failed to explode. The gun was reloaded, and a second shot fired. This time, the man with the binoculars cried out: 'Yes, I can see it!'

It had slammed into the side of the hill, just above the Russian position. The insurgents put a third shell into the barrel and, correcting their aim, they fired again. This time it was a direct hit.

Through the binoculars they saw the explosion, and an enemy gun fly up in the air.

It was taking the group a good half hour to reload for each shot. By the time the third shell had been fired, the Russians had turned their artillery around to face Budafok. They started shooting back.

'Absolute big fire!' Pálos says. 'Bang! Bang! I reckon if they would have expert army personnel there, they could fire a shot every two minutes. In about five to ten minutes time, the sunny morning turned into a big fog because of the smoke of the explosions.'

By chance, the insurgents had set up their gun just over the ridge of the hill.

'So you know how it was? The shells either hit the side of the valley, or they went over the top of us!'

Scattered across the hillside were a few large houses, surrounded by orchards and gardens. The houses sustained serious damage from the Soviet shells, but the Budafok group was able to hold its ground.

The insurgents were at the bend in the road for around four days. László Budaházy headed home every night – he would eat something and then collapse exhausted into bed. His sister worked at a factory that slaughtered fattened geese, for export to England. At the start of the uprising there were thousands of live animals in the factory, but no facilities to keep them for more than a few days. So every evening, Budaházy's sister would bring home a fifteen kilo goose in her knapsack.

'And you know, that was so expensive in Hungary, for years we never had one! But in those days, everybody ate their fill with goose.'

Budaházy's mother would cook the goose up, and wrap two large legs in paper. She would give the parcel to her son to take to the Balatoni út the following morning, as if he were setting out on a school excursion.

'It doesn't matter if your hand is dirty,' Budaházy says, 'and you don't need bread or anything. You just take it and eat some. Actually, it smelled like gun oil a bit, thanks to the hand grenades!' He shakes his head, scarcely able to believe it now. 'It was such a time, you know. It was such an extraordinary time.'

After three or four days, the Russians sent a column of six tanks up along the Balatoni út from the airfield at Budaörs. The insurgents, still dug in at the bend, spotted them winding their way up the hill. It was obvious who the Russians were coming for.

'We were holding a meeting as the tanks were coming up,' István Pálos says. 'If we have an ability to fire a shot every half hour, they could eat us alive in ten minutes. We have machine guns and small hand grenades, which could dent the paint of a tank. There was very little we could do.'

The tanks were still advancing along the Balatoni út.

Reluctantly, the men decided they would have to abandon their position. They slipped down into the narrow residential streets of Budafok. The field gun was too cumbersome to move, but they dismantled the large machine gun and took the pieces with them, hoping to establish a new position somewhere lower down.

By this time, they were coming under fire from the Russians. Some of the group was caught in it, but Budaházy and Pálos managed to escape, along with most of the others. They had the advantage of knowing the terrain.

Pálos retreated with several other men as far as the *vöröskút*, the red well – a junction where five streets run into a small square. At the centre of the square was an old open well that gave the landmark its name. The men tried to set up the machine gun, in case the Russians followed them there. But one of the pieces was missing. There was no sign of the man who had been entrusted with carrying it.

'That person never find the place,' Pálos says. 'Or he didn't know to come there. So we had the machine gun without the firing mechanism.'

They waited anyway at the *vöröskút*, beside their useless gun; but the Russians didn't follow them down. After a while, the insurgents sneaked back up to the Balatoni út corner. There was no sign of the Soviets. They had used their tanks to push the field gun over the hilltop and sent it crashing down into the valley. Then they had turned back.

It was the middle of November. Without the gun, there was nothing more that the insurgents could do. They maintained their armed patrols for a week or two, but effectively the resistance in Budafok was over. In the evenings, István Pálos would sometimes climb the steep stone steps to the higher parts of the district, and gaze out over Budapest. Across the river in Csepel, the fighting was continuing.

'It was like watching fireworks – you could hear the big rapid-fire guns, and see the explosives going all night long.'

But by the second half of November, even Csepel had fallen silent.

Although the fighting was over, a general strike was still in place. Vili Schmidt's father, Schmidt senior, was Budafok's representative on the Budapest Council. Every day, he made the journey into the city. Imre Nagy's government had ended, with Nagy seeking refuge in the Yugoslav embassy. The new pro-Moscow Kádár régime was negotiating with the Council to end the strike. While negotiations were still taking place, the insurgents held out some hope for change.

But then, around 27 November, Schmidt senior returned to Budafok with bad news.

'Sorry, boys,' he said. 'It's all over. Now they gonna line up everybody, pick us off one by one. Best we all go.'

Budaházy and Pálos knew they had to leave.

THERE IS one more story that László Budaházy has to tell me, before he moves on to talk about his escape. One day at the end of October, during the lull in fighting, Budaházy had run into his old enemy – police lieutenant Ersai. Budaházy had never forgotten the beating he had once received from the lieutenant, and his promise to kill him, if ever their positions of power were reversed. Now, in the central square in front of Budafok's Town Hall, his chance was about to come.

Budaházy was on patrol, a member of the armed guard set up by the insurgents. His pistol was tucked into his belt. When he caught sight of Ersai, he pulled it out. Ersai also saw Budaházy, but he didn't try to run. He must have realised there was no chance of escape.

Budaházy went up to the lieutenant and shoved him roughly to the ground. He cocked his pistol. Ersai was on his knees before him. Budaházy pushed the gun up against the lieutenant's nose.

'Ersai, you are going to die now! If you believe in your Communist God, you pray; because this is your last minute!'

Just as Budaházy was about to fire, the lieutenant suddenly began to weep. He lifted his right arm into the air.

'I hit you with this hand,' he cried, 'And look at it!'

Budaházy stared at the lieutenant's hand. There were no fingers on it. Ersai explained that he had been put to work as a spy in the Budafok tyre factory. One day, some of the factory workers had found him inspecting the equipment. They started up the machinery and it came down hard on his fingers, slicing through bone and flesh.

'I hit you with this hand,' Ersai declared, holding up his stunted palm. 'And look what God did to me!'

'And I just couldn't kill him,' Budaházy says quietly.

We are at the dining table in his spacious, airy house. It is a cold and windy Melbourne day, but inside it is warm, and that is not the reason for the shiver that has run along my spine. Budaházy's eyes are difficult to see behind his tinted glasses. I look instead at his wife, Suzanne, sitting quietly opposite him; then across the room to the wide picture windows, to a view of large new houses built on gentle hills.

'I let him go,' Budaházy says. It is as if he still can't quite believe it. 'I just couldn't kill him. He said: "My little daughter – for my little daughter's sake…" Maybe he was lying, I don't know. Look, I'm not a professional soldier – when you're a soldier, you're supposed to kill. You are ordered and you have to carry it out. That's easy. But when you're not a soldier and you kill, that's your own responsibility. And you have to live with it.'

He tells me a story about his elder brother, who was an army officer in the Second World War, and fought for four years on the deadly Russian front. His brother was one of the very few who returned home. After he got back, their father asked him one day to catch a piglet and kill it for their dinner.

Budaházy's brother grabbed the piglet, and took the knife in his other hand. Then he hesitated.

'I can't do it,' he confessed eventually.

Their father was incredulous. 'How come you can't do it? You're a soldier! How many Russians you killed in the War?'

'I don't know how many I killed, but this is different! This is different, I can't do it. If you make me kill, father, I'd rather go away from home.'

Budaházy's brother couldn't harm the piglet, even though he knew his refusal wouldn't save the animal's life. Their father took the knife and did the job himself.

'That's the way it is, you know,' Budaházy says to me now. 'That's why I couldn't kill Ersai. That was different. That was different.'

SÁNDOR TÓTH, who had always loved guns and wanted to be a detective, was quick to sign up for his local armed patrol. It was those final few days of October, when the fighting seemed to be over. Tóth strolled through the streets of Kőbánya, a police rifle slung over his shoulder.

In his chaotic Melbourne living room, Tóth stands and traces a diagonal line across his chest, demonstrating how he carried the weapon. The safety catch was always left off.

'I just had to lift it up and put the other hand to it to shoot, if I had to.'

He was heading with his patrol group one day up to the *éles sarok* – the 'sharp corner' – a place where the main road through Kőbánya sweeps past rail yards in a broad curve. The insurgents had set up a powerful 125mm anti-aircraft gun on the bend, blocking the main eastern approach to the city. Tóth and his group had been patrolling the area, and were circling back.

'I was walking on the right side of the footpath and, blimey Charley, walking there all of a sudden was this man.'

Tóth recognised him immediately. It was the former Party Secretary at the Kőbánya state brewery, a cruel and vindictive man. Tóth remembered a social event held at the brewery, where the Party Secretary had noticed someone dancing in a modern, western way. The Party Secretary took the unfortunate man outside and gave him a beating. Afterwards, he came back into the dance hall with a smile on his face, and calmly went to wash the blood from his hands.

'It was a blind corner there,' Tóth says, 'a truck storage depot, and he suddenly walked out right in front of me. With one of the Swiss caps, a long yellow raincoat on him, and rubber boots. And then he saw me. I never saw a man – it was a satisfaction, in a way – so scared. He knew me, and he knew that I knew him. And the disappointment in his face – he thought he was gonna get shot.'

The Party Secretary slipped his hands into the pockets of his raincoat and kept walking. Tóth was sweating, privately battling his own fear.

'I was watching his hands, and as he was walking towards me I knew there was a gun in one of his pockets. I held my rifle up.'

The Party Secretary was also sweating now. His face reddened, and he seemed to be on the verge of tears. The two men drew closer. When they were level, they gave each other a slight nod.

'*Jó napot* – good-day,' murmured the Party Secretary.

'*Jó napot kivánok*,' responded Tóth. He walked on past.

'I was praying to God,' Tóth explains now, 'I hope none of the other fellas know him. Because I would have been in trouble.'

The insurgent walking immediately behind Tóth ran and caught up with him.

'Who was that fella?' he asked.

'Oh, he's just a bloke who lives up here.'

His colleagues had no idea that they had just let a high-ranking Communist official slip through their grasp. Tóth shrugs lightly. He doesn't seem to regret the decision he made.

'So you can call me a Communist collaborator, in a way; but I didn't want to see the man killed in there – because what the hell for? I just didn't want to. Partly because I am a Christian. And maybe it was in my blood – I'm not a revenge seeker.'

But with that act of mercy, Tóth knew his card was marked. The Communists had seen that he was involved and, if the uprising failed, they would come looking for him.

Tóth tried to stay optimistic.

'They kept saying on Radio Free Europe – they were the biggest liars walking on two feet – they kept saying just to keep up the fight, and we shall be coming.'

There were already those who didn't believe it. An acquaintance of Tóth's had earlier told him: 'Nothing will come out of this, because the Russians will crush it all.'

Tóth shakes his head, and laughs. 'They bloody well did it, too!'

Early on the morning of Sunday, November 4, Tóth was on sentry duty in Kőbánya, guarding the gates to Csajkovszkij Park. A large section of the park had once belonged to the brewery, and the Dreher family who owned it had built a magnificent home for themselves there. The grounds included a castle-like building, a swimming pool and an open-air theatre. When the Communists nationalised the brewery, they turned the Drehers' home into a park for the people. Now the insurgents were occupying the buildings.

'All of a sudden, I heard this terrible rumbling,' Tóth says. 'I thought it was an earthquake at first. Then I realised that the Russians were coming.'

Before long, Tóth could also make out the distant booming of heavy guns. The noise would continue for most of that day. He rushed up to the *éles sarok*, where the insurgents were dug in at the corner. A column of Russian tanks was approaching from the north. A group of Hungarian soldiers, operating the anti-aircraft gun, was trying to stop them from coming in. The powerful detonations shook the local houses. Windows blew out, and chimneys came crashing into the street.

The terrified local residents took shelter in a series of deep cellars below the *éles sarok*, accessed by a cobbled driveway wide enough to take a truck. The cellars, built in the sixteenth century during the Turkish occupation of Hungary, were used for growing mushrooms. They also provided a source of cold, crystal clear spring water for the brewing process, and their constant, cool temperature was perfect for maturing and storing the brewery's lager.

The freedom fighters managed to hold off the Russians at the sharp corner for several days. Then, one morning towards the end of that week, they heard the unmistakeable repetitive beat of a helicopter's blades. It was coming in from the north. An Army lieutenant fighting alongside the insurgents had with him a set of powerful binoculars. He raised them to his eyes.

'It's a surveillance helicopter,' the lieutenant reported. He was a ginger-haired man with a bushy moustache. 'They're looking for positions, they want to see where we are. There are Russian officers in it.'

The helicopter circled overhead, its blades whirring, before heading back the way it had come.

As it disappeared, total silence fell.

'All of a sudden,' Tóth says, 'we heard whistles. I knew immediately what it was, because they'd done it in the city, too – they were firing with mortars. The most deadly mortar is a spread type. When it hits the ground it doesn't explode in a funnel, but it explodes like a grass cutter, big chunks of steel. It takes everything with it. And they began to fire the whole corner with these mortars.'

Tóth threw himself to the ground and crawled as fast as he could towards the cellars. The driveway of the cellar entrance was about fifteen metres below him. It was a sheer drop. Tóth lowered himself over the edge of the incline and, clinging to bushes and other undergrowth to stop from falling, scrambled halfway down and held himself there, tight against the embankment.

'I was safe, but I could hear the screaming and everything upstairs. It only lasted for about eight minutes, and it was all over. When I got up, we had anything up to twenty or so dead.'

Tóth is matter-of-fact. He doesn't describe the details of the scene at the *éles sarok*. There had been more emotion in his voice when he told me about the Jewish man who died near the Radio. Perhaps that man's death was more difficult because Tóth had been talking with him just before he died. Or perhaps there is less intimacy in twenty dead, because the mind cannot take in even such a relatively small number. I wonder how many people would have to die for my own feelings to shut down.

The insurgents carried their dead and wounded to a nearby foundry. Cleaning up the workshop, they turned it into a first aid room. Those who had survived the attack were badly shaken. Many of them decided it was too risky to stay on, and went home. By this time, the sound of whirring blades could be heard again, coming from the same direction as before. Tóth went back to the *éles sarok* and stood beside the ginger-haired lieutenant. They watched the helicopter fly towards them.

The lieutenant was distraught. 'We should have had the bloody thing shot down in the first place!'

The roar of the helicopter grew louder. The lieutenant gave his orders to the gunners.

'Lower the gun now, and get the height of the barrel up.'

The helicopter kept coming, closer and closer.

The lieutenant murmured to himself: 'You just come, you bastard. You just come!'

The helicopter passed over them, heading for the brewery. The gunner tracked it with the barrel of his weapon. The lieutenant ordered final adjustments for height and, when the helicopter was directly over the brewery, gave the instruction to fire. The machine burst into flames, splitting apart in the air. Large chunks of burning metal came crashing down into the brewery yard, the flames threatening to spread to the stores of flammable alcohol. The local fire brigade had to race to put them out.

The insurgents rejoiced. But one downed helicopter was not enough to turn the fight around, and Tóth knew it. He sensed the end was coming.

On Friday 9 November, the freedom fighters lost their battle for Kőbánya. The Russian tanks rolled through the *éles sarok* and rumbled along the streets of the district. They overturned the insurgents' anti-aircraft guns, and crushed their stocks of ammunition.

That afternoon, Tóth was on the first floor of one of the Party buildings close to his home, helping to defend it. The freedom fighters had piled sandbags up around the building, and had their rifles at the ready.

But their guns were useless against tanks. All they could do was watch helplessly as, outside, a Russian tank trained its barrel on their window, aiming directly into the room.

Everything moved in slow motion. Tóth headed for the doorway, feeling as though he were dragging his feet through molasses. He saw the tank fire, as easily as a machine gun.

Tóth was out of the room now. He swung onto the stairway. As he raced down the stairs he heard the explosion and a rush of air came from behind, the pressure of the blast picking him up like a rag and hurling him down one storey, slamming him into the ground. He lay still for several minutes. His body hurt all over, and he was somehow soaked to the skin with water. But he was alive. Around him, the building lay in ruins.

'Bugger it,' he thought. 'That's the end of it for me.'

He dragged himself up and, in a great deal of pain, staggered the short distance home. Everything that he had done over the past three and a half weeks flashed through his mind. The Communists knew that he had a gun. He was listed with the National Guard, he had a certificate to prove it.

'Tomorrow morning,' Tóth told his father when he reached home, 'I am leaving.'

He dug out his National Guard certificate and threw it away. Now Tóth wishes that he'd kept it, as a memento of those days. Because when he fled the country, he brought nothing out with him, and in the long, lonely years of exile had only his memories to sustain him.

THE NUMBER 28 tram deposits me at the *éles sarok* and continues on, rumbling around the sprawling brewery until it is out of sight. I am stranded in the middle of the wide, curving road. Trucks, buses and cars thunder past. The air is sour with diesel fumes. Behind me, a network of rail tracks converges to cross a concrete bridge. Ahead is a small, shabby shopping strip, clinging to the inner curve of the roaring highway.

The lights change and I cross to the shops, battling a fierce wind that hurls dust into my eyes. A ruddy faced man with a large, black moustache is coming the other way, swaying slightly as he walks. As he draws near, he calls out: '*Hey, bébé!*' I ignore him, and follow the road as it curves towards the brewery, which is now back in private ownership, part of the South African brewery group. The Dreher family has never returned, although the factory bears their name again. I pass pubs and discount beer outlets, the smell of hops strong even in the middle of the day.

Here I find the steep-sided cutting where Sándor Tóth took refuge from the mortar attack. At its base is a broad cobbled laneway that leads into the blackness of a cellar entrance. Glancing back, I realise for the first time how elevated this section of the road is, with an outlook north and west to the Buda hills, blue with distance. But the traffic is deafening, not conducive to admiring the view.

I turn instead into Maláta utca. This narrow street, which branches off the main highway, takes me into another world. The row of old Dutch-gabled houses has a rural feel. The cobblestone
156

street runs behind the brewery – visible behind a white fence are brick chimneys, and the ornate brewery and fermenting house, decorated in pastel colours. From it comes the gentle hum of machinery. Somewhere close by, a cock crows. Although I can find no sign of the foundry where Sándor Tóth helped to bring the wounded, it is easy to imagine myself suddenly back in 1956.

The illusion is broken when I round the corner, and am suddenly faced with squat grey 1960s apartment blocks. Keeping to the backstreets, wandering towards the centre of Kőbánya where I will catch the tram back into the city, I accidentally stumble across Csajkovszkij Park.

The municipal and Party buildings that Tóth once guarded are now back in private hands. Rust-coloured corrugated iron fencing separates them from the diminished park. On the white pedestal of a bust of Chopin someone has scrawled, in black spray paint, the initials of the local football club. At one edge of the park, two teenage boys are perched on the back of a bench, gazing intently at the road. Their anoraks flare out behind them. They look like brooding eagles, great dark wings folded along their backs.

I am not sure there is much here that Tóth would recognise any more.

Budafok, the southern district where István Pálos and the Budaházys grew up, is a similar blend of the old and the new. Using their memories as a guide, I climb a long, steep set of steps cut into the limestone hill. In this higher part of the district, there are things that seem familiar from their stories. The houses on either side are set in large gardens; dogs bark behind fences as I pass. In one place the rough stone steps are crumbling away, and I have to move to the edge, coming up close against a wire fence. The Alsatian on the other side flies into a frenzy, salivating over the wire.

At the top of the hill, the Balatoni út curves around an S-bend. I come out at the sharpest point of the curve, into a wide rest area where cars can pull off the road. Fifty metres away, two men are standing with their backs to the highway, urinating companionably into the bushes. At the other end of the rest area, a woman parades up and down beside the road. She wears high-heeled boots of white leather, her buttocks peep out from beneath black hotpants. She attracts the occasional blast of a horn from the busy road, but no one pulls over.

I turn and face north, looking back over the steps I've just climbed, searching for the view described to me by István Pálos. It is mostly obscured by a tangle of small trees. Still, through the branches I can make out the pale tower blocks of Kelenföld stretching in a long line across the valley, and beyond them are the walls of the Citadella on top of Gellért hill.

Perhaps the bushes have grown more dense in fifty years. The apartment blocks are relatively new. Otherwise, this is the scene that Pálos, Budaházy and their friends would have surveyed from their position at the highest point of the road. The barrel of their anti-tank gun would have been directed at those distant blue hills. A small group of men, with minimal military training, pitted against the tanks and firepower of the mighty Red Army. Certain of defeat, but determined to fight on anyway.

In 1956, one small window of opportunity opened to the West. Hungary wanted independence, it wanted to liberate itself from the iron grip of Communism. For a few short days, the West had a chance to help Hungary realise its dreams. And if it had, it's possible the rest of Eastern Europe would have quickly followed.

The invitation to change history came on 1 November. Imre Nagy, disturbed by the reports of Soviet troops pouring in across the border, sent an urgent message to the United Nations. Using a direct teleprinter connection to New York, Nagy declared

Hungary's withdrawal from the Communist Warsaw Pact. He asked the UN to recognise his country's neutrality, and help in its defence.

For the West, it was an unprecedented entry pass into Eastern Europe. But the timing could not have been worse.

Three days before Nagy's teleprinter message, Israel, Britain and France had invaded Egypt, due to a dispute over the Suez Canal. The Suez crisis took precedence over Hungary as far as the UN was concerned. Over the next few days, the UN Security Council and General Assembly were locked into hours of urgent meetings, but Hungary was barely mentioned. Nagy's plea for help fell like a whisper into a gale.

On the afternoon of 4 November, the UN General Assembly at last condemned Russia's actions in Hungary. But by then, Nagy had already made his final radio broadcast. The Soviet tanks had overrun Budapest, and a new, Soviet-approved government – headed by Kádár – was in place. Any attempt to enforce the UN resolution after that would have meant direct conflict between Russia and the West. And America, at least, was not prepared to go that far.

Instead, a Special Committee was set up to investigate the events of those few weeks in Hungary. Kádár's new government refused to allow UN observers into the country; but the investigators interviewed 111 witnesses, refugees who had made it to the West. Those raw and vivid testimonies provided the basis for the Committee's conclusions. The final report, which ran to 150 pages, was approved by the UN in June 1957.

'What took place in Hungary,' the report stated, 'was a spontaneous national uprising, due to longstanding grievances which had caused resentment among the people.'

In a departure from the restrained language used throughout the rest of the report, it went on to say: 'The Committee cannot but conclude that the Hungarian resistance to the second Soviet intervention was a heroic demonstration of the will of the Hungarian people to fight for their national independence'.

The report returned to calm, colourless understatement for its final judgement of the Russian action: 'A massive armed intervention by one power on the territory of another with the avowed intention of interfering in its internal affairs must, by the Soviet Union's own definition of aggression, be a matter of international concern'.

But it was too little, too late – concern would not help Hungary. The window into Eastern Europe had slammed shut months before, and the Cold War rolled on.

FROM THE start, eleven-year-old Tony Ámon, the boy who liked to play with toy soldiers, noticed that the second phase of fighting was fiercer, much more violent and destructive, than the first. The Russians had set up their heavy artillery positions in Buda, and were shelling Pest from across the river.

The Corvin Cinema, close to the Ámons' apartment, was one of the Russians' main targets. Deep explosions reverberated through Tony's apartment building. He fled with his family down the back staircase, taking refuge with the other residents in the cellar.

The front section of the cellar was blocked off, filled with seashells which belonged to the button factory across the street. In the rear area, each family had a space allocated for the storage of firewood and coal. This is where everyone congregated. It was close and confined, suffocating and humiliatingly public. During the worst of the fighting, there were at least a hundred people down there in the dark, crowded into the narrow corridor that ran between the containers of coal. They sat on stools and benches that they had brought into the cellar, with small bags of valuables – jewellery and important documents – by their side.

The adults were prepared, they had been through it all before during the air raids of the Second World War. But for Tony, everything was exciting and new. There were no toys, and the space was too cramped to play games, but he and the other children did not have a chance to get bored. They watched, fascinated, as the adults organised the details of their extraordinary life in the cellar. Several people fainted and had to be taken care of;

the sewerage became blocked and it took a full day to clear. Meals were prepared by candlelight, from the supplies people had with them: smoked bacon, *kolbász* sausage, and lentils, beans or peas with a little lard on top. Everything was heated over a small petrol-fuelled stove.

The time spent living in the cellar was a great adventure for Tony. He never worried that he might be in any real danger. Not, that is, until the first Tuesday in November.

Early that Tuesday afternoon, the area came under the heaviest bombardment of the uprising so far. The cellar was not designed as an air raid shelter – it was built for the storage of fuel, and wasn't deep enough to afford any real protection. It was not even fully underground – the street level ran at about the height of a man's chest. In addition, a vacant site on the northern side of the building left one long external wall utterly exposed. A direct hit on that wall would have brought the building crashing onto the families' heads.

The deep pounding from the Russian shells seemed as though it would never stop. Everyone knew the neighbourhood around them was being blasted into ruins. They were all waiting, terrified that the exposed wall would be hit.

'Somehow, somebody gave the advice that we should all stand up. Not sit through it, but be ready to move – I don't know where. So we were standing during that time.'

Ámon remembers his fear, and that of the adults. They were not to know that the building's vulnerable wall did not face in the direction of the firing. They held themselves stiffly upright, silent and tense, for an hour and a half until the shelling finally stopped.

The fighting continued for a few more days afterwards, but it would never again be so close or so threatening. Then one evening, while the families were still gathered in the cellar, they heard a banging noise from the rear wall. It came from behind the coal that was piled up against the bricks. Several of the men in the group

162

moved towards the wall and started to shovel the coal away. As they worked the pounding grew louder. Eventually shouts could be heard as well. Soon they could distinguish the words:

'*Fegyveresek itt, és át akarnak menni!*' Freedom fighters are here, and they want to come through!

A group of insurgents was trapped in the cellar of the building behind, and they were looking for a way out. On Tony's side of the wall, the men immediately started chipping away at the brick. From the other side, the revolutionaries did the same. Eventually a hole was created that was just large enough for a person to squeeze through.

Running along the wall beneath the hole was a drainpipe. It had been built over with brick steps – three up, three down. Another pipe ran parallel to it, at about head height.

'So they climbed over one by one,' Ámon says. 'A chap was standing there, and to each of them he said: "*Három lépcső, fejre vigyázz!*"'

Three steps, mind your head!

'At that time I was sitting at my place, and I just heard this: "*Három lépcső, fejre vigyázz!*" Rhythmically, as they climbed down.'

It was repeated twenty times or more, the sound of freedom fighters in retreat. The sound of hopes brought crashing down.

The following day, the families emerged from their cellar. They were able to witness for the first time the devastation that the shelling had caused. The majestic buildings and streets of the neighbourhood had been transformed into a wasteland of rubble. Burnt out military vehicles littered the road. A fog of brick dust enveloped everything.

In the Ámons' apartment there was a violation of another kind. While they had been in the cellar, during a quieter moment of the fighting a Russian tank had pulled up outside. The crew had climbed out and made their way to the first floor of the building.

The entrance to the Ámons' apartment, a set of tall double doors, opened from the stairwell. One of the Russian soldiers placed his boot at the centre of the doors, the weakest point, and kicked his way in.

'I saw the mess,' Ámon says, 'What the Russians did in the home. They behaved the same way that I had heard they behaved during the Second World War. They didn't use the toilet —' He hesitates, before continuing. 'They just did what they had to do in front of it. In front of it, on the floor; and used linen to wipe themselves.'

They had also taken food from the pantry, as well as socks and warm clothing. There was no jewellery in the flat; but Tony's grandfather's brass theodolite and sextant had disappeared. All the drawers were pulled out, and everything was mixed up together.

Worst of all for Tony, his own bedroom had not been spared.

'My toys were ruined. They trampled on one of my painted gypsum animals, and some toy soldiers. It was shocking to me – that my personal items had been ruined by them.'

Outside, the clean up had begun. Stooping in the street in front of his apartment, Tony inspected the kerb. It had been shattered by two tanks he had seen from his window the week before, approaching from the telephone exchange at Mária Terézia Square. The first tank had been a dark green T34; the other was a light yellowish-green colour, with a rounded turret. They had moved rapidly along the street, sliding heavily on the steep camber. The weight of the tanks had crushed the paving into fragments of stone.

Tony's school in Prater utca had been used as a hospital by the Corvin cinema insurgents. Outside it, the piles of rubble were growing. Some of them were already as tall as Tony himself. Then he noticed a strange, sweet smell. He looked more closely at the pile of debris nearest to him. A dismembered leg was standing upright, at the base of the heap. There was a short boot still

164

attached to the leg, but nothing above it. Tony realised what the smell was.

'It was *hullák*. Corpse smell.'

The stench of rotting flesh. It would be some time before it disappeared.

In spite of everything, hope stayed alive for a little while longer. At first, Tony went around his neighbours' apartments, knocking on their doors and telling them: MÚK! *Márciusban újra kezdjük*. In March – the anniversary of the 1848 revolution – we will begin again. It was a popular slogan at the time. Then his parents found out what he was doing, and stopped him.

He continued with his toy soldier games. Now, his best soldiers were named after the United Nations, while the ugliest ones – those trampled under the boots of the Soviet soldiers – became the Russians. '*Itt vannak ENSZek!*' Tony would say in his games. 'The UN troops are here!'

But in real life, the United Nations did not arrive. Meanwhile, the exodus had begun. The Ámons, listening to Radio Free Europe, heard a string of announcements from those who had made it across the border. There were requests to tell relatives in home villages that their loved ones were safely in the West. For the Ámons, and the others who were left behind, each new message only cemented their despair.

And at the entrance to the Ámons' apartment, the mark of a Russian soldier's boot remained firmly imprinted in the paintwork of the door.

EXILE

IT WAS DECEMBER, 1956. In Erdőhorváti, no strangers had been discovered approaching along the rough dirt road that led past the cemetery gates, where Péter Mándoki had organised an armed watch. But Péter felt anxious, nevertheless. In the capital, things were settling down. János Kádár had replaced Imre Nagy, and the hard-line Communists were back in control. Péter knew he would be counted as an Army deserter and, sooner or later, they were bound to track him down. When that happened, he would be facing execution.

Then Péter's closest friend in the village, Öcsi Fodor, confided that he was keen to try his luck at the border. Öcsi's soft eyes and delicate features disguised a strong ambition: he burned with a desire for the better, wealthier life he imagined was possible in the West; and now here was his opportunity to try for it. His aunt had directions for a possible route out of the country – some of her other relatives had escaped that way a short time before, and they had left the instructions behind. But Öcsi knew how dangerous it was, and the thought of attempting it alone made him uneasy. He wanted Péter to go with him.

Péter thought it over. Reluctant at first, he finally agreed, although he realised they might have left it too late. After the flood of refugees in October and November the borders had been tightened, and the chances of succeeding now were low. The friends decided Christmas would be their best opportunity, with everyone hopefully distracted by the holiday. It was agreed. No one could be trusted with their secret; no one in the village was to know of their plans.

But now that he had made the decision, Péter could think of nothing else. His family moved around him, going about their normal business, oblivious to what was worrying him. Surreptitiously, Péter stared at the faces of his parents and his sister, Matild, trying to imprint them on his memory. His younger brother, Miklós, was away at school in Miskolc. He was planning to come home for the Christmas holidays, but there would be little opportunity to say goodbye. Péter began to take greater notice of the farm that he had grown up on, the other houses of the village, the stream where he had played as a child. He realised that he might never see any of it again.

A week before he and Öcsi were due to leave, Péter couldn't keep the secret to himself any longer. He told his family what they were planning to do.

His father tried to talk him out of it.

'If you're caught, we might never see you again!'

'If I stay, and everything goes back to the way it was, they will probably take me away. You will not see me then, either.'

His family remained unhappy with Péter's decision. But they could see that his mind was made up, and there was nothing they could do or say that would stop him from going through with it. They agreed to keep quiet about the plans. Other than Öcsi's aunt, who had the route directions, they were the only ones to know.

On Christmas Eve, in the evening, the traditional Mass was held at the Roman Catholic Church. The entire village turned out for it. Öcsi and Péter went along so that no one would grow suspicious. Their hearts were racing with a heady mixture of excitement and terror. Around them, everyone was enjoying the holiday celebration. Anyone glancing casually at them would not have been able to tell that their minds were not on the hymns or prayers, but already on the journey ahead. For the two young men, the end of the Mass could not come quickly enough.

As soon as it was over, they went outside, ready to leave.

In front of the church, Péter ran into his brother, Miklós. The younger and shorter of the two men, Miklós tended to compensate for his lack of physical stature by putting on an air of bravado. Yet there was nothing behind the façade. He had none of the quiet determination possessed by Péter. Miklós would eventually move to a small town just south of Budapest, but he would never travel as far as his brother.

'You're crazy' Miklós told Péter that night. 'Crazy to try and leave by such a route!'

Their father, already resigned to Péter's decision, pressed 400 forints into his son's hand. It was money he had been saving with the intention of buying Péter a new pair of winter shoes.

'If you spend it and don't manage to get out,' his father told him, 'then you'll have to do without the shoes.'

Meanwhile, Öcsi had gone on to his aunt's house to say goodbye. To his surprise, he found his younger sister, Anna, there. Until that moment, she had known nothing of her brother's plans. When Öcsi's aunt and uncle offered to walk the boys to the edge of the village, Anna insisted on going with them.

It was cold, and the ground was covered in a thick layer of snow. The boys had some food with them for the journey, and a five-litre demijohn of wine each. Other than the money that Péter's father had given him, they took nothing else.

The small group walked as far as the cemetery, where they stopped to say their farewells. Beside them, their ancestors' graves looked out over the white hills. Anna was distraught. Tears streaming down her face, she clutched at her brother's long, elegant hands, trying to hold him back.

When she realised there was no changing his mind, she pleaded with the boys: 'Take me with you!'

'We don't dare,' Péter told her gently. 'I wouldn't be able to stop worrying – what if something happened to you?'

None of them could have foreseen that Anna might have been safer going with them. They had no way of knowing that, several years later, she would move to an apartment in Miskolc with a faulty gas heater. The heater was slowly and silently poisoning the air. One night Anna would fall asleep with her husband beside her, and neither of them would ever wake again.

Nor could they predict that Öcsi himself might have been better to stay behind. Many years later, when Péter was reading an English newspaper, Öcsi's name would suddenly leap out at him – a familiar configuration of letters in the wall of foreign print. The article mentioned a serious motorcycle accident.

Rushing to the hospital in Leicester, Péter and my mother discovered Öcsi in a coma, the surgeons unable to operate while he was unconscious, even though the flesh on his left leg was gradually rotting away. A car had turned in front of his motorcycle. It wasn't Öcsi's fault, and there was nothing he could have done to avoid it. His bike slammed into the side of the car, sending him flying through the air. With no helmet to protect him when he landed, the doctors worried most about the damage that might have been done to his brain.

Öcsi eventually emerged from the coma, but it was too late to save his leg. They amputated it below the knee. But the gangrene kept on spreading, climbing higher. They operated again, cutting into Öcsi's thigh. Still it didn't halt the creeping decay. For a third and final time the doctors operated. He was left with little more than a stump.

Öcsi's brain injury, however, seemed to be not as serious as the doctors had feared. On a practical level, he could function much the same as before, and he was allowed to go home. Except that he appeared to have no inhibitions – all his social skills were gone.

There was nothing to reign in his bitterness. He became a raging, mean-spirited man, unleashing the full force of his disappointment and anger on those closest to him. He was filled with paranoia that his friends were after what little money he had. At the same time, he was always seeking to borrow from them. One by one, the people he knew fell away. After a while, my father also stopped going to see him.

That winter day by the cemetery at Erdőhorváti, all of those events still belonged to the distant future. All Anna could see was that the boys would not take her with them, and they would not change their minds about leaving themselves. Öcsi and Péter turned away from her and continued resolutely along the road towards the railway station.

Anna cried long after they had disappeared from sight. At last, her eyes red and sore, she returned home. As soon as her parents saw her, they realised that something was very wrong. At first, Anna refused to tell them what had happened. They persisted, not leaving her alone. Finally she broke down. Through her sobs, the story came rushing out.

Öcsi's father listened in disbelief. He raced into his yard and hitched the horses up to his cart, then rode out of the village, driving the horses as hard as he could, hoping to catch up with the boys and bring them back home. But he did not pass them on the road. When he arrived at the railway station, seven kilometres away, it was dark. Everything was closed down. There was no sign of Öcsi and Péter anywhere. He thought that he must have missed them, and that they were already on the train to Budapest. Despondent, he turned around and headed home, the horses dragging the empty cart.

Péter and Öcsi were not on the train, however. They had arrived at the station a little before Öcsi's father. Finding it shut down for the night, they realised they wouldn't be able to get a train until the following morning – Christmas Day. It was too cold to wait around, out in the open.

'I know a family who lives close to here,' Öcsi said. 'They'll let us stay with them until morning.'

By the time Öcsi's father came looking for the boys, they were safe and warm inside.

The two friends caught the morning train without any further problems. They even managed to get seats, although it was busy. With frequent stops, the journey took most of the day. When they reached the outskirts of the capital it was already evening. Péter stared out of the window, but the snow was falling, obscuring the city in a drifting dark veil.

The train pulled slowly into Keleti station. Péter and Öcsi climbed out and walked the length of the platform, towards the great arched window over the station entrance. For both of them, it was their first time in Budapest. The largest town of their district, Miskolc, hadn't prepared them for the immensity and grandeur of the capital. They stood outside on the broad station steps, taking in the sweep of the buildings around them.

Péter felt overwhelmed. The train they needed to catch for the border left from a different station, on the other side of the Danube. He didn't know how to get there. And there was no one in this city of strangers they could turn to for help.

SÁNDOR TÓTH abandoned his dream of becoming a detective on 10 November 1956. That was the day he and his brother, László, left Budapest. The fighting still continued in Csepel, south of the city, but Tóth knew it was only a matter of time before it finished there as well. For Tóth, the decision was clear. He had to leave before the Communists came for him. The Party official from the brewery had recognised him in the street – they knew he was involved.

László was nineteen. Taller and more powerful than his brother, even though he was a year younger, he had the build of a fighter. He had not been involved in the uprising. But he was eager to try for freedom in the West.

Their fifteen-year-old sister was also desperate to leave. She tried to follow her brothers, but László chased her back home. The boys were prepared to risk their own lives, but didn't want to take a chance with hers.

The brothers walked from Kőbánya into the centre of Budapest for the last time. The city was occupied by the Russians. Tóth remembered the Corvin cinema, where he had spent a day early on, and wondered what had happened to it. They dropped by on their way to Déli station.

'It was shot to pieces,' Tóth says. 'The buildings ruined by artillery fire.'

He wouldn't find out what had become of the insurgents until almost thirty years later, when he read a book written by Gergely Pongrátz, one of the Corvin leaders. Then he would discover what had happened to Falábú Jancsi, the soldier with the wooden leg.

175

'He was knocked out,' Tóth tells me, 'and he bled to death, because they couldn't get him to hospital in time.'

It had happened on November 4, the first day of the second Russian incursion. During that single morning, about forty of the insurgents were killed. Falábú Jancsi was hit in the right eye and leg. He died from his wounds around noon, his head cradled in Gergely Pongrátz's lap. His last words were an exhortation to Pongrátz to not let the Russians take the Corvin.

Sanyi and László continued on to Déli station, across the river in Buda. Over the short distance between the Corvin and the station, the brothers were stopped three times. Russian soldiers demanded to see their identity cards, and searched them for weapons. Tóth had left his guns behind, and had told his brother to do the same. It was not worth the risk – they could be shot on the spot.

When they eventually reached Déli, they discovered there were no trains running.

'So we began to walk down towards the Székesfehérvár út on foot. It's 110 kilometres to Lake Balaton. It didn't matter – I was a good walker.'

He was wearing a fire brigade officer's coat and a pair of ski boots. He had taken them from a government clothing store that he had guarded during the uprising. Tóth could have helped himself to some comfortable military boots; instead, he had picked out the expensive ski boots, because they were more fashionable. Now, he was beginning to regret that decision. The new boots were already rubbing his feet.

As the brothers approached the outskirts of Budapest, they were questioned and searched again, this time at a large encampment of Russian soldiers by the side of the road. Soon afterwards, they managed to hitch a lift in a civilian truck. It took them all the way to the provincial town of Székesfehérvár, where the trains were still operating. The station was chaotic, with a crush of people and long queues for tickets. The Tóths caught a train as far as Fonyód, a holiday town on the southern edge of Lake Balaton. There they were faced with a wait of several hours, for a train that would carry them closer to the Austrian border.

By this time it was evening, and cold and dark outside. The small station was full, and there was nowhere to sit. László seemed particularly restless. He paced up and down, trying to keep warm. Then three men entered the waiting room. One of them wore an expensive leather jacket. Their eyes swept over the crowd. Tóth felt uneasy; his skin began to crawl with warning.

'I knew immediately that they were police,' he says. 'I could see it, I know their attitude.'

László was standing by the door. Sanyi said quietly to him: 'We'd better piss off from here.'

László glanced at him, just as the man in the leather jacket turned his gaze on them. The brothers were dressed differently from the locals. Anyone could see straight away that they had come from Budapest. Tóth felt himself break into a sweat, despite the cold air.

'Don't you worry,' László told Sanyi under his breath. His voice was strangely controlled, without a hint of panic. 'We'll be all right.'

Even then, Tóth failed to guess what his brother was about to do.

The leather-jacketed man seemed to be the one in charge. He strolled up to László.

'Can I have a look at you.' It was a command, not a question. He ran his eyes up and down László, taking his time.

László glanced at his brother. Sanyi noticed that although the blood had drained from his brother's face, bleaching his skin, he was perfectly calm. László turned back to the leather-jacketed man.

'All right,' László said, his voice rising quickly, 'You want my identification, do you?'

Reaching under his coat, he drew out a heavy twelve-shot revolver and, before the other man had time to respond, raised the gun to the policeman's head.

'There, you bastard!' László cried. 'You'd better piss off now, or I'm gonna put it right up you!'

Tóth could only stare at his brother in disbelief. He recognised the gun. He had given it to László himself, back in Budapest.

'He'd had it with him the whole time! I didn't know – he never told me. What beats me is, we were searched four times! He had it underneath his armpit.'

A hush fell over the waiting room. They were all watching to see what would happen next. The three policemen turned white.

'László meant it. I know if the fellow would have reached for his pocket, he would have pulled the trigger straight away, for sure! His brain would have spilt everywhere in there. Because László could shoot, too.'

Everyone was holding their breath. Then, without a further word, the policemen turned and strode out of the building, disappearing into the night.

Sanyi turned to László. 'We'd better walk out ourselves,' he said, 'because they gonna bring more fellows in with them now.'

László put his revolver away, and the brothers stepped outside. It was dark and completely quiet. There was no sign of the three policemen anywhere. They retreated a short distance from the waiting room, keeping close enough to ensure they could still hear the train when it came. They still planned to get on board.

It was freezing out in the open, but the brothers didn't dare go back inside. It was difficult to keep track of time, and Tóth couldn't be sure how long it was before the train eventually pulled into the station. The policemen had not reappeared – no one had come looking for them in the dark.

The brothers climbed up and settled into a carriage. It was a relief when the train started, and they left Fonyód behind. But they

178

hadn't been travelling for long before they were forced to disembark once again. The train had arrived at the small transit town of Türje, northwest of Lake Balaton, and it wasn't going any further.

Tóth discovered there would be another train leaving later for the main district town of Zalaegerszeg, a few kilometres further to the west. But the train wasn't due until late that afternoon. Impatient to reach the border, Tóth was disheartened by the prospect of another long wait.

'I'm not gonna sit here until then,' he thought. It was broad daylight; the locals would notice his clothes, and might call the police. He didn't want to risk it.

There were two other men at the station who had been involved in the uprising, and they were also heading for the border. The brothers had met them on the train. Together, the four men decided to set out for Zalaegerszeg on foot. It might not have been any faster than waiting for the train, but it felt safer than sitting around. All they had to do was follow the rail tracks. They scrambled down the embankment and set off along the tracks, out of sight of anyone passing on the road above.

Tóth began to worry about László.

'I could see on him, he didn't like the whole idea. And I wasn't happy with it, either – because I had these ski boots on, and my feet were hurting like hell. They were already full of blisters. Nevertheless, I kept walking.'

But after a while, László called a halt.

'I'm not going on any more,' he said. 'Let's go back to Türje, and wait for the train.'

But Tóth was not prepared to return to Türje. He had been directly involved in the uprising, whereas László had not. The consequences would be worse for him if he were caught. Then there were the two men's clothes: in his expensive boots and fire brigade jacket, Sanyi stood out. László was wearing an ordinary coat, he was not as conspicuous.

So when László insisted on turning back, Sanyi refused to go with him. I ask if that was a difficult decision for him to make.

'No,' Tóth says. 'I am a very practical man. When it comes to something, I choose the sensible way.'

László turned around, while Sanyi continued on to Zalaegerszeg with the other men. The distance between the two brothers increased, hour by hour.

After three days of steady walking, Tóth and his two companions reached Horvátnádalja, a village on the Rába River at Hungary's western border. They were tired and hungry. It was the middle of the day.

They followed the railway bridge over the river, and climbed up the scrub of the embankment to come out on the main road of the village. They had entered by the back way, thinking there would be less risk of being noticed. But as they emerged onto the street, an elderly woman standing in her yard saw them.

'You're from Budapest, aren't you?' she called. 'You're revolutionaries, aren't you? Come in quickly, before they see you!'

Tóth and his companions exchanged glances. The elderly woman seemed harmless enough – and she might be able to tell them how to get across the border. They followed her inside the house.

The woman gave them some food. While they were eating, she said: 'You want to get across the border, don't you? Well, you can't get across now – it's daylight. And you've got to know your way.'

Close to the village ran the Pinka River, twisting its way along the borderline. The area around the river was mostly swampland. It would be difficult to negotiate without help, especially at night. Then two young men arrived at the house. They were locals, and they offered to guide Tóth and his friends across the border.

180

'You will have to wait for sunset,' they said. 'When the fog settles down.'

The young men left, promising to return when it was dark.

One of Tóth's companions, János, took down the elderly woman's address. He told her he would write to her once they were safely over the border. In the evening, when the young men returned, Tóth and the others handed over all their money.

'We don't need it any more,' they said, 'Now that we're going to Austria.'

The five men left the house together. It was dark. A thick winter fog had settled close to the freezing ground. They walked in single file, the two guides leading the way.

They went through a pine forest and emerged into a large, open meadow. The grass was sodden with dew, the drops of water glistening in the moonlight. They started out across the meadow, heading for a clump of bushes in the distance. Beyond the bushes was the Pinka River.

'When we get up there,' one of the guides said, 'that's the border.'

Tóth thanked the men. 'You don't have to come any further.'

'No, we'll come up to the river.'

In his living room, Tóth leans forward on the sofa. 'That was their biggest mistake they ever done,' he says, before continuing with the story.

The men arrived at the bushes. In front of them was the river. It was perhaps only three metres across, but even in the darkness Tóth could see that the water was fast flowing. One of their guides pointed to a forest on the opposite bank.

'You see that?' he said. 'That's Austria already.'

Tóth stared into the water. He was still wearing his heavy fire brigade coat. With their clothes weighing them down, and the rapid current, he couldn't see how they would ever get across. But he wasn't allowed to consider the problem for long.

A reflector beam suddenly flashed on, bathing them in a strong, cold light. The source of it was to their right, not far along the river. The harsh sound of engines revving broke through the silence. Tóth heard the rattle of machine gun fire.

He didn't hesitate. Leaping into the river, the level of it reaching his chest, he began wading through the freezing water fully clothed. His two companions were beside him, but he suddenly realised the guides were still standing on the bank above. Tóth called out to the men, urging them to jump in, to make the crossing with them into Austria. The guides refused. Their families were at home, they said; they would be waiting anxiously for their return. They turned away and headed back towards the village. Tóth realised it was useless to call after them. He set his face towards the far bank, struggling against the current.

'We got across that river to the other side,' Tóth says. He makes the Pinka sound like a human adversary.

The opposite bank was steep, the undergrowth bushy. The men scrambled up one after the other. Tóth was the last out of the icy water, and his friends leaned down to give him a hand. Reaching level ground, he saw that they were in another meadow, with thick clumps of bushes scattered across the grass.

Across the Pinka, on the village side, two armoured cars were racing along the bank, firing wildly with their machine guns. The cars pulled up at the spot where the three men had jumped into the water. Tóth and the others ran quickly away from the river, putting some distance between it and them before crouching down among the bushes in the meadow. Shivering in their cold, sodden clothes, they waited for the firing to stop.

A long time seemed to pass before the armoured cars finally backed up and pulled away. The sound of their engines diminished into the distance.

The three men emerged cautiously from behind the bushes. The cars were definitely gone. They raced across the meadow into the safety of the pine forest. As they reached the trees they heard a prolonged burst of machine gun fire behind them, coming from the direction of the village. The sound was some distance away – whoever the firing was for, it was not aimed at them.

In among the pines the night was darker than ever. Fearful and confused, Tóth tried to remember what the guides had said about the border – were they in Austria now? He wasn't sure. They kept walking in the direction they thought the guides had pointed. The moon appeared from behind a cloud, and the men could see light reflecting off water. They had arrived at another section of the Pinka River. They knew it wound back and forth between Austria and Hungary. But which side were they on?

A narrow walking track ran beside the water. The men decided to follow it, and at first it seemed to take them the way they wanted to go. Then suddenly it changed course, curving off in the wrong direction.

János grew anxious. 'We've got to cross the river again,' he said. 'If we go that way, we're going back to Hungary!'

Tóth stared along the Pinka. For some distance ahead, he could see the moonlight sparkling on the water. Then there was only blackness. He assumed this meant that the river wound back on itself. He thought that if they kept following the track, they would probably end up on the right route again.

But János refused to listen. He insisted they cross the Pinka. At thirty-five, he was the oldest in the group, and the other two tended to defer to him because of it.

Reluctantly, Tóth lowered himself once again into the icy, fast-flowing water. This time, it was a little easier. The river came only to their waists, and it did not take them long to wade through it.

There was a steep hill on the far side, followed by a hard climb through dense shrubs that reached their shoulders. Arriving on a ridge, they saw that the ground fell away to an unsurfaced road below. The recent tracks of heavy vehicles were visible in the dirt.

In the distance, there was the glow of electric lights, and the sound of dogs barking.

'You hear that?' Tóth said angrily. 'That's the border guards' dogs. We are in the border, on the Hungarian side!'

János shook his head. 'I don't believe it.'

Tóth himself prayed that he was wrong – none of them wanted to face the possibility they might have to cross the border all over again.

Nauseous with anxiety, they scrambled down the hillside to the road. From there they had a clear view over the area. Deep in the valley below them was a brightly lit compound. There were Alsatian dogs, and large wire fences. Armed men in uniform walked about under the lights. That kind of security was found only on one side of the border. The Austrians weren't concerned about who came across.

Tóth was furious.

'Bloody hell! I told you, didn't I? We have to get into the bush straight away – down that way. We're in the wrong spot altogether!'

The men headed for the cover of a lightly forested area, and pushed their way through the shrubs and trees. The fear, the darkness, the bitter cold were never-ending, it was like being trapped in a nightmare and yet it was real, and there seemed to be no prospect of ever waking from it. All they could do was keep trudging towards the elusive border.

'My feet was hurting like hell. We'd been walking about three hours. Soaking wet. And freezing cold. But it didn't matter.'

They arrived at another clearing. Tóth looked cautiously around, and saw two watchtowers, a few hundred metres away.

'Look, you silly bastard,' he said to János. 'You see that?'

There was no doubt about it – they were on the Hungarian side. They would have to cross the border again.

The three men crept towards the nearest watchtower, keeping low. They needed to find out whether anyone was in it. If there was someone on guard, they would be spotted as soon as they tried to cross. They wouldn't stand a chance.

When they reached the tower, there was no sign of movement from it. One of them climbed up to make sure. It was empty.

Ahead was the *nyomsáv* – the cleared strip of land at the border that was often laid with landmines. Beyond it in the distance, about three hundred metres away in the dark, Tóth could see bushes.

'And I knew the river was there again – that terrible river! But I was more scared of the strip of land, the minefield. We thought we'd better just run across and see what happens, and don't think about it. And we walked across in there, and nothing happened.'

They reached the bushes. As Tóth had suspected, the Pinka river was in front of them. They had already been over it twice, and it seemed it was not finished with them yet. The three men stood at the river's edge, contemplating the water. It looked very deep at that particular spot. Even so, Tóth could see that János wanted to cross it again. But this time Tóth was determined to avoid it.

He stared along the shining surface of the river, and thought he saw a bridge, a few hundred metres further down. In his exhausted state he knew it might be just wishful thinking, a chimera based on a trick of the moonlight.

Trying to sound more confident than he felt, he said: 'Look, János – I guarantee you, if we walk down along the riverside, on this side of the river, there's gonna be a little bridge.'

'Oh, there's no bridge in here,' János said.

But this time, Tóth held his ground. The three men made their way down the river.

'And sure enough,' Tóth says gleefully, 'there was a narrow and a simple bridge. So we walked across the bridge.'

On the far side of the river there was another walking track, and the men followed it for a while until it veered off in different direction. Then they decided to cut across a ploughed field instead. The earth had soaked up the recent heavy rains, and turned it into deep mud. It sucked at their boots, making hard, slow work of walking. Almost two hours later, they noticed a cluster of structures looming out of the darkness ahead. They went up for a closer look.

'It was an old cemetery,' Tóth says. 'We walked into the cemetery and looked at all the names – and they were all Austrian! German. And we must be in Austria. Because until then, János wasn't quite sure. Actually, I was getting that tired, I was getting to the point where it didn't matter *where* I was any more!'

During the four days since he had left Budapest, Tóth had snatched only a few short bursts of sleep. Frozen to the bone, and starving, all three men were teetering on the edge of confusion and delirium. They stood in the cemetery for several minutes like punch-drunk boxers, unable to think through their next steps. Then they started walking again, in the same direction as before. It was all they knew how to do.

All of a sudden, ahead in the distance, Tóth noticed an electric light.

'I don't care what's in that direction,' he said to the others, 'I'm going that way.'

They advanced through the thick mud, their feet aching with sores and blisters. It was another half an hour before they covered the distance. Scrambling down a steep embankment, they found themselves on a long, wide stretch of bitumen road.

They were delighted. A road like that meant civilisation; it meant towns where they could find food, warmth, and a place to rest. The light Tóth had seen glimmering in the distance came from an electric lamppost, suspended over a large, white board. There was a single word printed on the board.

It was the name of a town: 'Hagendorf'.

WHENEVER I mention to people that I am interviewing refugees, they are always interested. Sometimes they ask: 'Are they grateful for the opportunity they were given?' This loaded question always leaves me floundering for answer. I've started responding with people's stories.

In Austria, Sándor Tóth stayed with the men he had crossed with for a while. One of them, János, wrote to thank the elderly woman who had helped them in Horvátnádalja. She wrote back, and that was when they learned what had happened to their guides.

The two young men had turned around at the Pinka river and headed back towards the village. They were just ahead of the Russian armoured vehicles. The Russians had pulled up at the riverbank but, seeing that Tóth and his companions had already crossed and were out of reach, they turned back and pursued the two guides instead. On foot, the men had no hope of outrunning the Russians. The vehicles were firing at them, and there was nowhere to take cover. One of the young guides took a dumdum bullet in the leg. The bullet destroyed so much tissue and bone that the limb later had to be amputated. His friend was shot dead beside him.

In Budapest, Tóth's father was also made to suffer for his son's freedom. The Communists brought charges against him, and he was sentenced to two years in jail. They took the view that he should have been able to prevent his sons from leaving.

But there was some good news. Tóth's brother, László, crossed the border safely. He had caught the train to Szombathely and arrived in Austria sooner than his brother. He went to America, where he still lives now.

Tóth went first to England. His trade certificates were still in Hungary, so he couldn't look for similar work. He learnt English and decided to study nursing. It might have been a long way from his dream of becoming a detective, but Tóth was happy enough.

After eighteen months in England, he decided to move to Australia.

'The Cold War was so tense that everyone thought war will break out any minute,' he explains. 'And the Russian Army back then was very strong. They were worried that the Russians might run over the whole of Europe. That is why I thought I'd better leave. Because Europe is a terrible danger, it's always just war, and war.'

Australia appealed to him because it was as far from Europe as it was possible to get. Tóth continued his nursing studies at Melbourne's Austin Hospital. But he did not find Australia a very welcoming place. On his weekends off, he was at a loose end. He wasn't interested in cricket or soccer. If he went to the movies he would be sworn at for being a foreigner, and young Australian men would try to pick fights with him. Tóth longed for the late night coffee houses, the vivid nightlife of Budapest that he had left behind.

'In comparison to that, Melbourne was like a funeral parlour!'

One Sunday morning, wanting to cheer himself up, Tóth travelled into the centre of Melbourne. He headed for the motorcycle shops along Elizabeth Street.

'I wanted to buy a motorcycle to go to work. I would always have loved to have a motorcycle – at home it was an impossible dream to get one, and in here, it was possible. And there were the most beautiful machines there.'

The shops were shut because it was a Sunday, but Tóth was happy just window shopping. Then a policeman approached Tóth, while he was gazing at the bikes. The policeman had a large, burly build, and towered over the slight-framed Tóth.

'Come on, you little fellow,' the policeman barked. 'What're you doing here?'

'Nothing, sir,' replied Tóth.

'Why are you here?'

'I'm looking at the motorcycles. I want to buy a motorcycle.'

'But why are you here today?'

Tóth shrugged. 'That's what I'm doing.'

'You shouldn't be here,' the policeman told him brusquely. 'You'd better piss off home now, or I'll run you into Russell Street. I think you're bloody well loitering!'

Flustered and angry, Tóth had no choice but to move on.

Back at the hospital, Tóth's relations with his co-workers were not going well either. There was a swelling undercurrent of resentment against him.

'They begin to grumble and carrying on: "Here comes the bloody wog". I didn't even know what a wog was until later on. They said: "He's getting his days off, Saturday and Sunday, and we have to work during the weekend!"'

Tóth was astonished when he heard that. He had thought the others were choosing to work weekends because the pay was better – time and a half for Saturdays, double time on Sundays. As a new employee, he had assumed the lucrative weekend work wasn't available to him.

He approached the charge sister.

'I said to her, if they want, I can swap with them. "Oh, would you, Mr Tóth?" Would I hell! And sure enough, they changed. I was earning up to ten pounds more in wages.'

It's not surprising, then, that Tóth turned to Melbourne's Hungarian community for friendships and a social life.

In the late 1960s, the freedom fighters were granted amnesty by Hungary. This meant Tóth was able to visit his homeland for the first time since he left, and see his parents and sister again, without fear of imprisonment. The last time he went back was in 1974, when Kádár's Communist régime was thawing, but the uprising was still frowned on as a 'counter-revolution'.

I wonder if he has ever felt tempted to return for good, now that democracy has returned to Hungary and the Fifty-sixers are regarded as heroes.

Tóth shakes his head.

'Some of the things that are happening over there today are a disgrace. Because nobody ever lived out on the street – begging and that kind of thing was completely prohibited. I noticed when I was in there last time that young girls of 14 and 15 years of age are offering themselves for pleasure. For money. The Communists wouldn't have tolerated that – no way! So they can have their freedom and their so-called democracy!'

In 1956, Tóth fought for a dream of freedom. The reality, when it finally came, fell short of his expectations. The Hungary that Tóth left behind no longer exists; and the country that has replaced it is alien, its culture and values entirely foreign to him. But this is not the only reason that Tóth no longer thinks about returning permanently to Hungary.

'I have my loyalties to this country,' he says.

He seems to mean that he is settled here, has found his place. When he tells me that his sister, who stayed behind, is better off than him, there is no trace of regret in his voice. And although the dream he once cherished of becoming a detective has long since faded away, he still has a strong interest in rifles. He indulges it at his local shooting range with his son Frank.

190

More than most people, Tóth is able to be happy with what he has.

His two smallest sons are sitting with us in the room, watching *Grease* on television. Olivia Newton-John has squeezed herself into tight black leather when I feel I am ready to leave. I stare at the tattoo on the knuckles of Tóth's right hand – letters in faded indigo ink spell out his name, *s-a-ny-i* – and realise with a jolt that I'm not listening any more. Tóth is still talking, his story seems to have no end – it has no structure at all.

I pack away my notebook and tape machine, and stand up.

Tóth also slowly rises, but the flow of his words doesn't pause. As we move towards the kitchen, Tóth shows me a clipping from a Hungarian newspaper, which hangs framed on the wall.

'This is the notice of our marriage – in Hungary, in 1974.'

The last time that he was there. The slightly yellowed page displays a photograph of the bride and groom. Tóth's hair is thick and dark, his direct gaze full of confidence. His bride looks much younger than him.

'We knew each other for three days,' he says. More of the story aching to be told, but not to me, not tonight.

Mrs Tóth and two more of their children are clustered around a table that fills the kitchen. They have been keeping out of our way. Mrs Tóth's face is clean and shining, as if she had spent the evening bending over steaming saucepans. She smiles at her husband.

'How is your throat?' she asks, using English for my benefit.

It is late, and Tóth has talked continuously for over three hours, but he simply shrugs. His eyes are sparkling. He is animated, youthful – it is as if he has regressed to the age of the groom in the photograph. Or younger still: to the twenty-year-old who fought on the streets of Budapest. I am the one who is exhausted; emotionally drained and aching for bed.

Tóth follows me out into the sharp air of the yard, apparently reluctant to let me go. He doesn't seem to notice the cold. I am shivering. My face, I know, will be hollow and creased, my skin bleached and dry as paper.

Like Wilde's *The Picture of Dorian Grey*, I have taken on Sándor Tóth's history and grown old tonight; while he is a young man again – strong, and light on his feet.

ACROSS SOUTHERN Road in Heidelberg West, a short distance from Sándor Tóth's home, five interlocking coloured rings hang suspended above a narrow road. Set into the footpath that leads to the small shopping centre nearby is a design of a flaming torch. Next to it are the more modern buildings of Olympic Village primary school, while along by Darebin Creek, bicycle tracks wind through Olympic Park.

It has been a day of heavy showers, and the wet road sparkles in the brilliant sunshine. As soon as I arrive with a friend at the old Olympic Village, dark clouds appear, and the rain hammers down. We drive slowly along the quiet streets between the park and the school, peering through the windscreen wipers at the widely spaced brick houses and two storey flats. The gardens are lush and green, but on one of the houses a window hangs loose, and several others are in need of a fresh coat of paint. The area has the neglected look of a public housing estate – a place where people care about their homes, but there isn't the money to maintain them. An elderly woman in a beige raincoat struggles home with her shopping, but I see no one else on the streets. A low, grey sky makes everything look bleak.

Trying to get my bearings from a hand-drawn map downloaded from the internet, I search for the houses built for the athletes in 1956. Some of them have been demolished and replaced, but many still remain. I assign countries to buildings as we round another corner – the Philippines, Romania, Japan.

It was the year the world came to Melbourne.

But at the opening ceremony for the XVI Olympiad, held on 22 November, six nations were missing. Egypt, Lebanon and Iraq withdrew in protest over Suez. Spain, the Netherlands and Switzerland refused to take part because of the Soviet action in Hungary. The Soviet Union was represented though, their athletes parading through the Melbourne Cricket Ground. Their officials arrived on a large white ship, the *Gruzia*, which docked in Port Phillip Bay. Its three swimming pools, and first class cabins decorated with wood panelling and gold velvet curtains, were widely reported in the Australian press. And despite the turmoil at home, a delegation of one hundred Hungarians also made it to the Games.

With the help of my map, I think I have found the house the Hungarian team used. It is one of the originals – a wide, two-storey, pale brick walk-up, arranged diagonally across its corner plot. I remember reading about the confusion over which flag should be flown in the Village – the original, Communist, version was torn down by an angry crowd of local Hungarians, assisted by some of the team.

The rain has eased slightly. I get out of the car with my camera, and head for the pavement opposite. There are grey net curtains in the large, square windows. Behind one of them, someone must be watching – as I take my photographs, a dark-haired woman comes to the front door. She stands on the step in the open doorway, watching me. For a moment, I consider wandering across to explain why I'm here. Perhaps she will ask me inside. But her face is hard and suspicious, not at all inviting. The weather is worsening. I run back to the car, and throw my camera on the back seat. Rain batters the windscreen as we drive away.

A few weeks before the opening ceremony of the Games, the Hungarian athletes were sequestered at a training camp in the mountains outside Budapest. They were close enough to the city to hear gunfire, and see the smoke rising. Some of the athletes suspected then that they might never see their families again.

When they started out on their long journey to Australia, via Czechoslovakia, the fighting was not yet over. As world-class athletes they enjoyed certain privileges, such as the opportunity to travel to the West, fast promotions, and exemption from the normal duties of military service. Yet the majority had no fondness for the régime, and were firmly on the side of the insurgents. On reaching Prague, many of them signed their names to a declaration of support for Imre Nagy's new government, and sent it back to Budapest. They were full of hope; there was still a chance they might return to a liberated homeland.

By the time their plane landed in Melbourne, Hungary had lost the fight. Imre Nagy was gone. János Kádár's government was in place. The news was broken to the team during the flight.

Exhausted and dispirited, concerned for their families, the athletes filed off the plane. They were welcomed by a group of around a thousand local Hungarians. The crowd wore black armbands, and carried a Hungarian flag draped with black ribbons. At the sight of the athletes, they began to sing the slow and melancholy rhythms of the Himnusz. Mournfully, the athletes joined in.

December 6 was an oppressive, sticky day. At 31ºC, it was one of the hottest of the Games. It was a Thursday afternoon – a working day and not yet the finals, but the Olympic pool stadium was packed nevertheless. Local Hungarians crowded the stands. They had come to watch Hungary's water-polo team, the defending champions, pit themselves against the Soviet Union. The sides were playing for much more than an Olympic medal.

The teams lined up for the start, fourteen men in the water, facing each other across the pool. Numbered caps with ear guards covered their heads tightly. Beneath the surface they wore only trunks, and their bare chests shimmered in the pale underwater light. The caps of the Hungarian team were white; the Russians' dark. Lined up at each end of the pool they were like pieces of a chess set, the forces of good against evil.

The starting whistle blew. The two teams sprinted towards the ball, which floated at the centre of the pool. Lifting themselves high out of the water with powerful kicks, the players hurled the ball through the air one-handed, or flicked it to teammates across the surface. Bodies collided, players traded blows and kicks. Water polo is renowned for its brutality, but this game was always going to be worse than most.

The seven-minute quarters dragged by, with frequent stops for injuries and fouls. As time went on, the violence increased. The crowd roared with pleasure as the Hungarian team pulled away, quickly scoring four goals one after another, two of them by the young, confident player Ervin Zador. The Russians seemed to have no answer.

Then in the final quarter, with the ball at the far end of the pool, Zador briefly risked taking his eye off his opponent, Valentin Prokopov. Prokopov rose out of the water and struck Zador on the side of his face. The punch gouged a deep gash over Zador's cheekbone, just below his right eye. Blood poured from the wound and spread through the water. There was one minute left on the clock.

The Hungarians in the crowd turned wild. They rose from their seats, spitting and shaking their fists at the Russians. Some of the spectators tried to reach the poolside area. The referee had no choice but to blow his whistle, ending the match early. The Hungarians were declared the winners, to loud cheers from the emotional audience.

Zador swam to the edge of the pool, and was helped from the water. His tall frame towered over the Olympic officials. Blood streamed from the gaping wound on his face. It trickled under his chin and traced a vivid, watery line down the centre of his dripping chest. The Russians walked away from the pool under a police escort, to protect them from the furious crowd. All around the world, the newspapers printed the black and white images of Zador emerging from the water.

'We felt we were playing not just for ourselves,' Zador said later, 'but for every Hungarian. This game was the only way we could fight back.'

Politics was spilling into sport. The organisers of the Games grew increasingly uneasy about the legacy it would leave. Then a seventeen-year-old apprentice carpenter, who lived with his family in the centre of Melbourne, had an idea. From his window, John Wing would watch filmgoers filing quietly and neatly inside the cinema next door. They would come out later merged into one excited mass. He wrote to the Games organisers with his suggestion.

At the closing ceremony, for the first time in Olympic history, the athletes did not parade separately in their national teams. Everyone walked freely in the packed stadium, all countries mingled together, smiling and waving at the excited crowd. It was to become a tradition of the Games.

But by then, twenty Hungarian athletes had been forcibly taken on board the *Gruzia*. Many of the remaining delegation, including Erwin Zador, hurriedly applied for asylum. The Australian government, anticipating the possibility of defections from Communist countries, had chosen to take a low-key approach. Perhaps fearing it might detract from the Games, they refused to consider any applications until they were over. The Olympic Organising Committee, on the other hand, was concerned for the safety of the Hungarians at the Village. Acting on its own initiative, it established an armed guard. The government angrily had the guard withdrawn.

In contrast, the United States wanted to encourage defections. Its government issued public statements, assuring Hungarians they were welcome to seek asylum in America. Zador, along with the majority of the defecting Hungarians, ended up in the US. Only eleven of the team applied to stay in Australia.

File number 1606/4, of the Australian Department of External Affairs, contains details of interviews held with the asylum seekers. The file is stamped 'SECRET', in green stenciled letters. The front page holds the file's subject, handwritten in a curling script with ornate capitals: 'Political Asylum: Hungarian Olympic Team in Melbourne'.

The interviews are sparsely written, but the voices of the athletes still come through. There are glimpses of the hard lives of turners and fitters, men who had worked since the age of twelve. There was a father who died in Bergen-Belsen, and another who had been in prison and suffered bad health. What comes through most of all in these brief descriptions is a strong disillusionment with Communism. A yearning for a different future, a different kind of life.

Then there are the stories of loved ones left behind – the barest of details, hinting at more. Wives, children and parents. A five-month-old baby daughter, a first child, left in the care of her young mother in Budapest. There are cablegrams from Vienna, passing on joyful messages from husbands and wives who had made it safely across the border. And messages travelling the other way, seeking news, the terse language of the cables still conveying a deep sense of desperation.

Compared with the barely contained emotion of the cablegrams, the official comments on the file are shallow and condescending. 'He is a fine type of young man and showed no sign of fear … a good future seems to be assured him.' There are no reflections on the knife-edge decision the athletes are making – the tension between hope for a new life, and fear for those left behind. Instead,

198

there is an assumption that, of course, the defectors should welcome the opportunity. An implication that the West is granting them a favour they can never repay.

In all, forty-five Hungarian athletes, almost half the team, would not return home once the Games were over. Nor would another Hungarian man, part of the delegation, who fell from a bridge over railway tracks into the path of an oncoming train. Officially, it was called suicide.

But in the euphoria of the closing ceremony at the Melbourne Cricket Ground, the athletes walked side by side, all nations together, in an ideal of how the world could be. The crowds waved and cheered, and the XVI Olympiad became known as the 'Friendly Games'.

IN 1993, TOWARDS the end of summer, my father visited me in Budapest. He slept on the fold-out sofa in my living room, a brief stopover on his way to Erdőhorváti. Each morning he rose early to put away the sofa bed, folding the blankets neatly, before I woke up. During the day, unable to fathom the complex transport ticketing system, he rode the trams for free.

'This elderly chap got chatting to me on the tram,' my father told me one night when I came in from work. 'He was complaining like heck! Unemployment, how expensive everything is, so much crime, all these foreigners coming into the country and taking things over. I didn't tell him I was a foreigner! He said things was better under Communism. He wanted the Commies back!'

The man on the tram wasn't alone. The very next year, the former Communists – who hadn't disappeared, only regrouped – would be voted back into power. It seemed people preferred to be looked after by the State, rather than having to fend for themselves. They missed the element of safety and certainty that went with the old régime, despite everything else it had entailed. But it was too late to turn the clock back. Any government would now have to work within a market system. And the loans provided by the West to finance that system had come with conditions attached – they included the winding back of welfare provisions, such as generous maternity leave. Hungarians didn't get the chance to vote on that.

In 1956, the West had made an unofficial promise to Hungarians – that it would help them overthrow Communism – and it had failed to follow through. Then throughout the 1980s, a second promise was made. This one was more subtle than the first. It came via television and film, rather than over the radio. But the outcome was much the same.

In Erdőhorváti, my relatives bought a television set. It took pride of place in the living room. The entire family used to gather in the evenings to watch it, while they digested dinner. The show that caused the greatest excitement was re-runs of *Dallas*, with JR Ewing's Texas drawl dubbed into melodramatic Hungarian. My relatives watched the dramas unfold, fascinated by the clothes, the mansions, the lifestyles that until then had been beyond their imagining.

Hungarians didn't think that capitalism would provide everyone with the wealth of an oil baron; but they did expect that their lives would improve. It was another promise that wouldn't be kept. Instead, many would lose their jobs and become poorer, while only a few would grow rich. Hungarians could not have anticipated the sudden chasm that would open between the extremes of wealth and poverty – creating a breeding ground for dissatisfaction, and an explosion in crime. But then, we in the West could hardly have warned them. Grown used to unfairness and inequality, it fails to shock us any more.

In Mr Horváth's apartment there is a small television. It looks incongruous among the old-style furnishings. I switch it on in time to catch a group of teenagers playing table football. One young man lifts up a scrawny cat, and deposits it on the table between the rows of plastic men. It is the Hungarian version of *Big Brother* – surveillance and social control turned into entertainment; all the fear of Orwell's words removed. The teenager tries to coax the animal into playing, but the cat lacks interest.

I also wait for it to be over. Next there is a piece about Hungary's acceptance into the European Union, a new phase of transition. The farmers are worried that they will be paid less for

201

their produce. Then a middle-aged man appears, answering the interviewer's questions. I don't understand all of it, but there is bitterness in his tone.

'The ones who left Hungary had it easy,' he says. 'Now they're coming back, spending the money they made in the West. They don't know how hard it was for those of us who stayed.'

Paul Marer, an academic, is one refugee who has come back. I find him at the Central European University's business school on Nádor utca, not far from Parliament House. The building has high ceilings, and a grand curving staircase with polished balustrades. Students clatter up and down, their shoes resounding on the stairs. Marer, a Hungarian-American, has a spacious corner office on the second floor, behind tall, thickly padded doors. He comes from behind his desk to greet me, and takes my coat. We sit on comfortable chairs arranged around a coffee table. It is calm here after the activity of the stairwell, but the room is insanely hot. I roll up my sleeves. Marer wears a light shirt. There are small beads of sweat on his round face.

With extraordinary clarity, Marer can point to a small number of events that were pivotal in his life. The first came when he was eleven, and he lost a foot in a streetcar accident. Then, a few years later, he read 'An American Tragedy' by Theodore Dreiser. Critical of the American Dream, it was the story of a young man driven to murder through the relentless pursuit of wealth and success. But it didn't put Marer off America. Instead, it made him long to go there.

'I thought if ever I had the chance to go to the US, I would not make stupid mistakes!'

The third major event came in 1956, when he was twenty years old. Because of his foot, Marer had not been required to join the Army. He was living with his parents in Budapest and working as an accounts clerk, unable to go to university because of his middle-class background. When the uprising began, Marer took no part in it.

His life would have continued as before, if it hadn't been for one small argument with his parents.

'I received a slap for something silly, like the shoes I was wearing.'

It was enough to change everything. Inflamed by anger, Marer took his winter coat and some money and, without a word to his parents, left the house. It was 7 November. He started walking towards the border.

At Esztergom, on the Danube northeast of Budapest, Marer was arrested. He had reached the town in the middle of a curfew, when no one was supposed to be out on the street. Soldiers took him to the military barracks. Marer boldly demanded to see the man in charge. He was presented to the commander of the barracks. Marer noticed that the commander's army insignia had been torn off his uniform and then hastily re-attached. The officer had been with the revolution. It gave Marer courage.

'I am related to the Chancellor of Austria,' Marer declared, 'and I have a message to take.'

No one was more surprised than Marer when the commander gave the order to release him.

He headed out of town, following the Danube westwards, heading for the Austrian border. Sometimes he got lifts; once, he climbed on a train that took him almost to the border town of Mosonmagyaróvár. He met three men on the train, and when they had to disembark they stayed together, for the final part of the journey. It was hard going, on foot across frozen ploughed fields, in the middle of the night. The weather was bitter. By then, Marer had been walking for five days. The pain from his amputated foot was almost unbearable. The men he was with helped him over those last few kilometres, one man supporting him on either side. They kept him going with regular swigs of rum.

Marer held out just long enough to reach Austria. As soon as he was sure they were over the border, he told the others: 'Leave me here. I can't go on any more.'

Austrian border guards picked him up, and took him to an infirmary. He spent three or four days recovering there, before being transferred to a refugee house in Vienna.

Marer had just one aim: to get to America. It was the land of opportunity, the country he had dreamed of since reading Dreiser's book. He queued in the long lines outside the US Embassy, sat through an interview and a medical examination. They put him on the second flight of refugees out of Austria. He arrived in America on November 23.

Marer was not disappointed by what he found. From the beginning, he immersed himself completely in American culture and language. He never once felt homesick, and he took no part in local Hungarian groups.

'There wasn't one in Florida,' he explains, 'And then I was busy with my studies. Although my experience with Hungarian communities is not good at all. Hungarians are notable for their disagreements with each other. If there are three Hungarians together in a room, they will have four different opinions.'

For the most part, Marer found acceptance, although not from everyone. In the winter of 1958, he was working in a Florida bank, handling cheques and checking additions. On New Year's Eve, late in the afternoon he was packing up, getting ready for the walk home. It was already dark outside. But before he could leave, the Bank's Vice President motioned him over.

'I'm sorry, Paul,' she said. 'We're going to have to let you go.'

One of the bank's customers had phoned to complain that he couldn't understand Marer's accent. Marer was dismissed with two weeks severance pay.

Overall though, Marer found the opportunities outweighed his negative experiences. He attended university – an option that had been closed to him at home. But Marer never completely forgot his background. It deeply informed first his studies and then his academic career, guiding his interests towards the Soviet economy, and particularly Soviet relations with Hungary. He was involved in the early discussions to establish the Central European University, with an office in Budapest. And as the régime eased, he made visits to Hungary, first as a tourist and then for business.

Finally, in search of a new personal challenge, Marer came to live in Budapest. He has been at the Graduate Business School for four years, and is as much at home here as in America. But now he feels it is time to leave.

'I am culturally more in tune with the US,' he says, 'More ready to accept US values.'

Although there are things about Hungary that he finds very satisfying.

'Personal relationships are deeper – and animosities, also! The US is more superficial. And the US is ahistorical – it doesn't care about the past, it only cares about the future.'

When he leaves Hungary, he wants to maintain links with the country. He concedes that one day, it's possible he might consider relocating here for good. But for now, his direction is clear.

'Still, I'm always asked: "Where are you from?" Regardless of whether I'm in Hungary or the US, I'm always 'from' somewhere else.'

I know how hard it is for me to accept the fact that I will always be a foreigner in my father's country. How much more difficult, then, to come to terms with being a foreigner in the place where you grew up? To always be an outsider, wherever you are?

We have been talking for some time. I arrived towards the end of the afternoon, and now the windows have grown dark. There are books and papers piled on Marer's large desk. I tell him I hope I haven't taken too much of his time.

'No.' He smiles broadly. 'Academics like to talk!'

He gets up and helps me put on my coat. Then, unexpectedly, he asks: 'Can I have a hug?'

I laugh. We embrace easily, with the warmth of old friends. The odd intimacy of strangers who have exchanged life stories.

After the heat of Marer's office, the street seems unbearably cold. I walk briskly past the Gresham Palace on Roosevelt tér. The grand old insurance building faces the Danube, its tall front windows overlooking the floodlit Chain Bridge. In the early twentieth century, its elegant rooms accommodated wealthy visiting clients of the insurance company.

Under Communism, the rooms were partitioned into small apartments and ordinary Hungarian families moved in. But, like the rest of the city, the building was left to decay.

Now the tenants are gone, ejected against their will, and the old Palace has reawakened. Spotlights pick out golden tiles. The façade gleams through the twilight, a soft beacon on a dull day.

This is the work of Béla Fejér, another émigré who has come home.

It was Marer who told me that the 1956 group of migrants has been unusually productive and successful. Studies have shown that they have made an enormous contribution in their adopted countries. Now some of them are returning to invest in Hungary's future as well.

It has taken Fejér seven years to restore the Gresham, almost twice as long as planned – that was what it took to reconstruct the ceramic tiles, marble staircases and statues, using original materials and traditional methods. There are wrought iron gates and stained glass, crafted with an attention to detail rarely seen any more. The project is a nostalgic look backwards to old Hungary, a monument to the past.

And yet it is also a step forwards. When the transformation is complete, the Gresham will reopen as a luxury hotel. Opulent rooms will open onto balconies with views across the Danube to

Castle Hill. It will draw the wealthiest of international tourists, bringing Hungary money and prestige. At around the time that the Gresham opens, Hungary will join the European Union. The Gresham will be a symbol of Hungary's new place in the exclusive club that is Europe. An elegant, prestigious building, restored to its former glory. And once again beyond the reach of ordinary Hungarians.

At Kálvin tér Metro station near the Museum, the homeless are laying out their beds for the night. The florist, newsagency and tobacco shop are already dark behind plate glass windows. Out in the main concourse, the men's faces are wan and blue-tinged under searing artificial lights. They lie beneath a row of public telephones, one man to a booth. Most of them have covered the grimy floor tiles with a piece of flattened cardboard. A rolled rag serves for a pillow. The telephones with their plastic booths hang over the men's heads, giving some sense of privacy and shelter. By contrast their torsos and legs, protruding into the concourse, look vulnerable and exposed.

IN HIS CALM, airy Melbourne living room, where classical music plays softly on the radio, the pastor János Dabasy places a thick lever-arch file on the coffee table. He is planning a long trip to Europe during the northern spring. The file contains brochures and postcards of the places he will visit, each one carefully numbered and placed in a plastic coversheet. As excited as a child, he leafs through them, pointing out specific things to me. There is a computer spreadsheet with every day of the trip mapped out. Hungary is prominent in the schedule.

'I hope to get a ticket for the opera,' he says.

This will not be Dabasy's first trip to Hungary; but it was almost forty years before he returned for the first time. Even after the Communist régime collapsed, he might never have gone back. It was only when his wife, Éva, received an invitation to deliver a lecture in Budapest that he considered it. After much deliberation, he decided to accompany his wife on her trip. It was 1994.

At the Hungarian border, confronted by the armed guards, Dabasy felt a rush of anxiety. But he told himself that there was no longer any danger, and they continued on into Hungary. When they reached Budapest, Dabasy wandered around with Éva, pointing out to her the places he remembered. In Kossuth Square, they stopped in front of Parliament.

'I was standing about here,' he told his wife. He turned his face upwards, towards the high windows of the stone buildings surrounding the square. 'The ÁVO started firing from there, and there.'

The couple walked on up to the Vár, tracing the maps of Dabasy's memory. There was the building that had once been his college lodgings, opposite the Hilton Hotel. Right there, in the doorway, one of his student colleagues had collapsed. Dabasy remembered how the young man had been losing blood, and was gasping vainly for breath. He had been shot through the lung.

That night, as he lay in his hotel bed, Dabasy had a vivid nightmare. He was a young man again, and back in the uprising. He lived through all the events once more – the sounds and images were unusually intense. He felt the textures of things, noticed smells, the full horror of it ran through him. He couldn't escape, couldn't wake up.

The following morning, Dabasy noticed something strange. Until then, he had always felt some tension in speaking about the uprising. Now, suddenly, it seemed easier to talk of his experiences. Physically also, he felt in better health than he had done for years, since leaving Hungary all that time ago. His nightmare was a release: a weight had been lifted from him.

Tony Ámon, the SBS presenter, had described to me in his mellifluous voice a dream that he used to have, after reaching Australia. He had escaped Hungary in 1975. At the time he was thirty years old, and married to a woman he had met at school. The marriage had broken down long before his escape, but Ámon had made a proposal to his wife: they would keep silent, keep up the pretence of the marriage, and not bother each other. That way, Ámon was able to get a passport to visit the West – the authorities believed he would be sure to come back, as long as his wife remained in Hungary. For her part of the deal, Ámon's wife got to keep their flat and the furniture.

The plan worked beautifully. Ámon went abroad with his newly issued passport, and didn't return. There was nothing the authorities could do.

Once he was safely in the West, Ámon's dream began. It recurred over several years, becoming gradually less frequent as time passed. In it, Ámon awoke to find that he was suddenly back in Hungary. His escape had been for nothing; he had inexplicably returned to his homeland again. As he lay on the bed, the full realisation of his situation pressed down on him. All the old tension and despair returned. His mind worked feverishly. He had managed to get out before. But how would he be able to do it a second time?

Ámon was not the only one to suffer this dream after leaving Hungary – other migrants had told him they experienced something similar.

'To me,' Ámon reflected, 'it means that we were feeling so trapped in Communism. Young boys always look up at aeroplanes going, and ponder about it – every aeroplane meant to us freedom passing by. Because whoever was on that aeroplane was free.'

For almost forty years, János Dabasy had been trapped. Physically, he had escaped the oppression of Hungary; but mentally and emotionally, he was still there. It was a dream he couldn't wake from. He needed to return to his country before he could feel completely free.

In 1956, János Dabasy had spent most of the uprising based at his college lodgings in the Vár. Messages came over the telephone from the university, instructing them to go to this place or that. One day, Dabasy was sent to guard Cardinal Mindszenty, the head of the Catholic Church, who had been freed from house arrest by the insurgents. He was in the capital for a few days, before returning to his cathedral at Esztergom.

Standing in front of Mindszenty's building, feeling proud to have been entrusted with such a duty, Dabasy suddenly noticed someone filming him and the other guards. He had no way of knowing if it was Western journalists behind the camera, or the

Communists. But when the time came for Dabasy to consider whether to stay or leave, he would remember that film. It would play a key part in his decision.

For Dabasy, the most wonderful aspect of the few short days between the two Russian interventions was the return of religious freedom. There was no longer any need to hide his beliefs. On Sunday, 28 October, he made the short walk from his college lodgings to the small baroque church at Bécsi Kapu tér, on the northern side of Castle Hill.

'I went to church, and I rang the bell.' Dabasy's eyes are brimming with guilty pleasure, his voice is rich with it. 'And the Russians came in: "What are you doing?" I said: "It's Sunday, I'm going to church." They were not happy, but they didn't do anything about it. They turned around, and I pulled the bell. I rang the bell!'

I imagine the sound pealing out across the city below, celebratory and joyful, the music of freedom and hope. An image in István Pálos's poem comes back to me: Budapest as one enormous church, the clear sky its dome, people bursting into song on its streets.

The emotion that gripped Budapest in those few days was like the euphoria of a fresh love affair. There was selective blindness – people mostly ignored the slight niggles that seemed to threaten their new existence, such as the reports of Russian reinforcements flowing across the border. In their optimism, the Hungarians believed their happiness would go on and on.

'I reckon if the United Nations had sent in some peacekeepers' Dabasy says, echoing the views of the other Hungarians I have spoken to, 'Hungary would have been free. Well, we were naïve, but we believed that they will come in and help. And if they would only send in just a handful of United Nations police – they don't even have to have a proper army – the Russians would not have come back.'

I ask Dabasy if he felt betrayed.

'Definitely,' he states sadly. 'Definitely. Probably if we would have had oil, or something like that – that would have been different. But unfortunately, we didn't.'

In the early morning of Sunday, 4 November, Dabasy was rostered on guard duty at his college lodgings. He could take a little time to sleep, but had to keep fully clothed in case something happened. Just before dawn he was lying on his bed, his gun ready beside him, when the message came through: 'Wake up the college, the Russians have come!'

Dabasy leapt up and went downstairs, first rousing the students in the building with the loudspeaker, then trying to reach the university by phone, to find out what they should do. He discovered there was no way to physically reach the other students at the university, because the incoming Russians had cut off all the bridges and main roads. Dabasy was told to head out to the Buda hills instead, and try to organise a partisan-style resistance from there.

Dabasy and the others set off for János-hegy, the highest of the hills on Budapest's western edge. In summer, it afforded refuge from the city, a place where residents could escape the cloying heat. But that day was icy and wet, with a biting wind. Even the long, strenuous walk did not do much to keep the cold at bay. They reached the peak around mid-morning, and took shelter from the damp, bitter weather in the *kilátó* – the lookout tower, which afforded panoramic views of the city below.

The day wore on towards lunchtime. There were about a dozen of them, hunkered down in the *kilátó*. There was nothing for them to do. The sound of explosions rose up from the city, and they could see smoke hanging low, but they couldn't tell how the fighting was progressing. The hours passed slowly. Dabasy grew increasingly restless. Eventually, he and a friend of his had had

212

enough. They started back down the hill, and spent the night with the family of another friend, who lived on the route into the city.

The following morning, the two men were approaching the Castle district when they heard sporadic machine-gun fire. The Russians were sweeping the road every now and then to keep it clear. The young men advanced cautiously. During a break in the firing, they reached the base of the Castle wall, on the western side of the Vár. They had to climb a long set of stone steps that snaked up the side of the brick wall. At the top was an arched stone gateway, walled in on three sides to form a small watchtower. The windows, crude gaps in the brickwork, provided a view across Buda towards the hills.

When they reached the gateway, there was someone waiting for them.

'There were these young little kids, about fifteen years old – the gun was bigger than the kid – guarding the Castle Hill at this gate. They were the Széna tér children.'

Széna tér was a small square close to the base of Castle Hill, on the Vár's northern side. A group of insurgents were operating out of the square.

Dabasy told them: 'Look, we are university students, we're in the National Guard. We live up there and we want to …'

'Have you got anything to prove it?' demanded the boys.

Dabasy took out his National Guard certificate to show them.

The boys put their guns down, and leaned them against the wall while they inspected the papers.

Dabasy chuckles at the memory. 'Both of them! If we were not friendly – a slap across the face, get the gun, and go!'

The boys let them through. The Mátyás church was directly ahead, and the college was just a few hundred metres away, along a narrow cobbled street. But the district was under heavy shelling from the Russians.

'You could hear the fire, and then the ssshhhhhhhh; and then when it hit, it exploded. So we run a few metres and ducked, because we didn't know where it will hit.'

It took a long time to cover the short distance to the college. When they finally arrived, the building was almost entirely deserted. There was no food in the kitchens. They quickly realised there was no point in trying to stay there.

For Dabasy, the discovery was disheartening. It was the clearest sign yet that his world had irrevocably changed. He would not be returning to the college, he would not be completing his studies. Even when the fighting was over, nothing in his life would ever be the same again.

Dabasy left Hungary on Sunday, 25 November – eleven days after Sándor Tóth had arrived safely in Austria. After finding the college lodgings virtually abandoned, Dabasy had stayed for a few days with his relatives in Budapest, then he had returned to his family home in the western city of Győr.

That Sunday, the entire family was gathered around the table eating lunch, when the telephone rang. It was Dabasy's uncle, who lived close to the border.

'If you want to go out,' his uncle said, 'come straight away.'

Dabasy and his family immediately put their spoons down, stood up from the table, and rushed to pack a few things. Only his grandparents had decided to stay – they felt it was too late in their lives to attempt such a change. Dabasy phoned his fiancée, Bea, who was still with her family in Budapest. He told her he was leaving, and urged her to join him.

'She didn't want to come,' Dabasy says. He repeats it, more softly this time: 'She didn't want to come.'

Reluctant as he was to leave without Bea, Dabasy felt that he had no choice.

214

'The situation looked hopeless,' he explains. There was the film that had been taken of him when he was guarding Mindszenty. 'So who's got that film? I was involved in the revolution. If they catch me, I would be one of those who end up in Russia.'

They are reasons enough to have left. But Dabasy seems desperate to justify his decision, and he keeps adding more. I get the feeling he is trying to convince himself, more than me.

'An enemy of the working class and got into university,' he continues. 'How did he get into the university? All these sort of things would have come up. So I could not stay. My honest belief – I was worried that if they ever catch me, I would be taken. If they caught me, I would not be here. In fact, we got the message from my grandparents in Győr that they were looking for us. After the revolution, when everything settled down, they were looking for us.'

With a flood of words, he is trying to push away the guilt that he still seems to feel, all these years later, for having left Bea behind. Dabasy told himself he would try to get his fiancée out afterwards, once he was safely in the West.

The family did not waste time packing cases. Dabasy pulled on an overcoat. He went to the cupboard in his room.

'In the cupboard I had two piles of socks: one to wear; the other for my grandmother to mend. And I had a pile of handkerchiefs there. So I got hold of my briefcase and put the socks in there – but not the good ones, the ones with the holes! I got hold of the handkerchiefs and I put them in there, too. Well, the socks with holes in I got rid of straight away. So in the end I had nothing else, just the old Hungarian handkerchiefs.'

Dabasy's uncle lived in Csorna, fifteen kilometres from the Austrian border. He had organised a guide to take the family across. But when they arrived, the Dabasys found that the man had taken another group into Austria one night, and hadn't come back. By this time, the flood of refugees was well underway. The Dabasys had to stay at a hospital in town, along with several other families hoping to make it to the West, while they searched for another guide. Fortunately, it didn't take them long to find one.

Just north of Csorna, the Hanság canal runs straight along the border. As at the point where Sándor Tóth crossed, the area around the canal is treacherous with swamps, and at night a thick fog often forms. But the Dabasys made their crossing in broad daylight, at three in the afternoon. The Russians couldn't use their tanks or armoured vehicles for fear of getting bogged in the soft ground. The real danger lay in the last five hundred metres before Austria, where the ground was cleared of vegetation, and laid with mines and barbed wire. Wooden watchtowers were posted at regular intervals.

But someone was looking after the Dabasys that day. Their guide led the family to a small narrow gauge railway, and from there they followed the tracks to a bridge over the Hanság canal. They crossed into Austria without any trouble. Had they waited until nightfall, however, as most of the refugees did, things could have turned out very differently.

'That night was one of the first really cold nights. Everything froze up. The Russians were able to come in. And on that bridge there were some thirty or forty people they killed overnight. So we were lucky that we crossed during the day.'

From Austria, Dabasy went first to Germany. He could have stayed there and continued his engineering studies on a scholarship, but his father had a brother who lived in Melbourne, and the family decided to move to Australia to be close to their relatives. As well, they had similar concerns to Sándor Tóth.

'We knew that we didn't want to meet the Russians any more, Dabasy says. 'They could have started off in breakfast in Vienna; and lunch in Munich. That fear was probably unfounded. But in those days it was very real.'

216

During his stay in Germany, Dabasy tried desperately to find a way for his fiancée to follow him out. But Bea was a Hungarian patriot of the old school. She believed fervently in the words of the poet Petőfi: Hungarians must live and die in their homeland. Even after Dabasy moved to Australia, he kept on waiting and trying, urging her to join him. But Bea refused to abandon her native soil.

For seven long years, Dabasy remained engaged to his distant love. In 1963, he finally gave up hope. The two of them agreed to break off the engagement. It would set them free to move on with their lives, if they could.

Dabasy later married – his wife, Éva, is a vibrant and intelligent woman. They had a daughter who grew up to be a classical musician: she has played French horn with the Melbourne Symphony Orchestra, and studied at the Music Academy in Budapest. Dabasy's work with the church gave him immense satisfaction. And in 1995, in an ecumenical ceremony, Dabasy was ordained as a pastor. It was one of his proudest and most happy moments. And yet, for much of his life, Dabasy carried the burden of his experiences with him. His memories were dark stones weighing down his soul.

'For a long time I have been thinking about whether I have done the right thing,' Dabasy says quietly. 'But I always come back to the conclusion: if I stayed home, I wouldn't have been helping anyone, because I would probably have been taken with the other 41,000 Hungarians to Russia. So there was not much choice.'

Yet he seems haunted by the possibility that exile is always a choice – even when the alternative is death. And his fiancée chose differently from him.

'That's the only thing – that Bea stayed home. If she would have come out, I would have been much happier. And life would have been different.'

For twenty years following their agreement to part, Dabasy had no contact with Bea. Then one day, out of the blue, Dabasy received a letter from a shared goddaughter. It had been posted to an old address, but it still somehow managed to reach him. The letter carried news of Bea.

'I found out that she never got married,' Dabasy says. 'That sort of hits you. Because you still have – and I still have – feelings for her.'

On his return to Budapest in 1994, Dabasy felt compelled to visit Bea. Filled with trepidation, but with his wife, Éva, to support him, the three of them arranged to meet. Dabasy's voice sinks to a breathless whisper as he describes that encounter – the first time they had seen each other in almost forty years.

'She was a wreck!'

So hushed, it is as if he can scarcely bear to hear it himself.

'A nervous wreck, shaking and crying all the time.'

As it turned out, Dabasy would never see Bea again – she had only a few years left to live.

We sit together in Dabasy's serene, white living room, with its view out over hills blue with distance. Classical music still plays gently on the radio. On top of a glass cabinet sit two plaster busts of composers – I recognise Beethoven, but can't tell who the other one is. A decorative plate with clock hands attached sits above the lintel that separates living from dining areas. A loud ticking measures out the seconds as they slowly pass.

AT THE END of November 1956, László Budaházy asked Suzanne to leave Hungary with him. She didn't hesitate – she said yes.

Suzanne had seen little of her fiancé during the uprising. While he was out fighting the Russians on the Balatoni út, she had spent much of her time at home with her parents. Stuck in the house, and with little word from László, her imagination ran free. She conjured all kinds of unpleasant scenarios about what her fiancé might be doing. Partly as a distraction for herself, she helped out in Budafok's hospital.

'I was afraid of the sight of blood,' she says shyly, her hands tucked inside the sleeves of her crimson jumper. 'But I helped with the bandages. That was from old bed sheets, they tore it apart. That was the only way I can help.'

Then at the end of November, László came around to Suzanne's house. He told her he was leaving. He didn't give her any time to think it over. But Suzanne didn't need time to think.

She gives a rueful smile. 'We thought we might come back in a couple of months' time.'

'We didn't think it's gonna last forty years!' her husband agrees. 'Maybe a couple of years – something happens, you know. Nothing happened.'

László broke the news to Suzanne's parents.

'We have to go,' he told them. 'The first chance we have, we get married, and that's it. I can't give you any promises – I can't even promise that she gets through the border alive.'

Her parents could see that her mind was made up, and they didn't try to stop her.

At five the following morning they headed into the city with another young couple, friends of theirs. From the city they caught a train going west, towards the border town of Mosonmagyaróvár.

'Didn't know where we were going,' Budaházy says, 'Didn't know what we gonna do. Just knew I had to get out before they catch me. Tried to hide for a while – I was sleeping for one night in my grandmother's place; and then where I was working. They tried to make a fake roster, that I was working all the time. But I knew it wouldn't wash.'

Unlike Sándor Tóth, who had left his weapons behind, László Budaházy took everything with him. He carried a pistol, and a machine gun hidden beneath his coat.

'And grenades,' he adds.

I stare at him incredulously.

'And two goose legs.' He laughs, pursing his fleshy mouth. 'That was in the pocket! We had nothing else. We didn't have a suitcase – you can't.'

Then he remembers something else.

'And a knife.'

He catches his wife's eye across the table.

'The only thing I promised her was that if we get caught, and the worst comes to the worst – I cut your throat so you don't get caught by the Russians. That's all.'

'That's all,' Suzanne echoes quietly.

It was after lunch when their train drew close to Mosonmagyaróvár. The conductor worked his way along the packed carriages.

'This is the last safe stop before the West!' he called, 'Everybody off!'

Budaházy took out the two goose legs. They were plump, expensive, force-fed geese from the Budafok factory where his sister worked.

'I told Suzi: "Honey, eat some, because you never have one like this ever in your life again". And we never did!'

'No, we never did.'

'Because they don't force-feed the goose in any other country.'

The four friends jumped off the train. There was no real station, only open fields. About two hundred other people got off with them. There was chaos as everyone tried to work out what to do. Budaházy felt uneasy. The noise from so many people might draw unwanted attention. The four waited for the main group to move away, allowing some distance to grow between them. Then they also started across the fields, heading westwards.

After a short time, Budaházy noticed a man in a policeman's uniform coming towards them. The man was armed with a machine gun. The uniformed man stopped to talk to some other people from the train, and then continued on. When he reached them, it turned out he was simply a local man, out hunting rabbits.

'What's the best way to go to the West from here?' Budaházy asked, as calmly as if he were requesting street directions.

'Will you believe me? Because I told those others not to go that way. There's gonna be trouble down there. The Russian guard unit's there.'

'Oh, I'll believe you,' Budaházy said. 'If you tell me wrong, I'll come back and cut your throat.'

'Okay. Sit down in the cornfield and wait until night. Then, that way…' the rabbit hunter pointed, 'You'll see lights – a village. That's Nickelsdorf. That's on the other side of the border.'

He warned them to avoid the main border crossing at Hegyeshalom, which would be on their right. About five kilometres further south, they would see a farm building. They should keep well away from that also, because the Russians were there. Between the farm building and Hegyeshalom, there were watchtowers with searchlights, and they would need to be careful.

'But,' the hunter said, 'the Hungarians won't touch you. The Russians – if they catch you, they'll take you.'

The four young people waited in the cornfield for night to fall. The crop had not yet been harvested, and they were able to hide among the tall stalks. When it grew dark, they could see the lights of a village ahead, as the hunter had promised. They began to move cautiously forwards. No one spoke. But they were not in total silence.

Budaházy bangs softly and rhythmically on the dining table with his open palm.

'We heard people, same quiet like us, going towards the west. I don't think they were further away in the dark than this window, but they never said anything.'

He strikes the table again.

'We could hear them coming. Maybe six, ten people.'

The steps faded away. Budaházy and his friends kept going. The corn gave way to a flat, ploughed field. It was a fine and clear night, the stars were out. It was bitterly cold. Then they heard the rattle of weapons being carried in front of them.

'That must have been Russians. They were talking, but we were too far away. We didn't understand what language they were speaking.'

The four waited for the soldiers to pass, and then continued. Suddenly, a searchlight flashed on. They threw themselves flat on the ploughed earth. The beam crossed right over them. They were pinned in its glare. They waited for the machine guns to start firing. But the beam moved on past, and the light went out.

Budaházy turned to the others.

'Let's run out of here as fast as we can!'

They got off the ground and raced across the field, towards the village. Behind them, the search beam clicked back on. The four friends kept going.

'We didn't think,' Suzanne says. 'We just wanted to cross the border and be safe.'

They didn't stop running until they reached Nickelsdorf.

László Budaházy gets up awkwardly from the table, and reaches for his wooden cane. Relying heavily on the smooth stick for support, he heads for a cupboard at the far end of the kitchen. He retrieves some photographs from it, and a cardboard tube.

Suzanne and I gather around as László spreads his memorabilia out on the kitchen bench. The centrepiece is an A4-size black and white photograph, protected by a clear plastic sleeve. Twenty or thirty young people pose for the camera, arranged in rows. My eye is drawn to the couple at the centre of the group. The photographer's light picks them out – their clothes are paler than the rest, and they seem to glow. It is the Budaházys.

Suzanne, in a white cardigan, is sitting. Thick, black hair frames her face; her expression is confident and bright. Her mouth is dark with the lipstick that her old workplace forbade her to wear. She gleams with the knowledge that she is free to make her own choices at last.

László stands beside her, recognisable by his precise mouth and high, arched brows. His delicate, lean face is quite beautiful – the only flaw is his closed left eye, undisguised then by tinted glasses. Even so, his gaze holds the camera's lens with greater intensity than any of the others.

Taken in Vienna that winter, it is their wedding photograph.

The people around them are the 'Golden Youth' of Budafok, gathered together again after safely reaching the West. Suzanne Budaházy leans over the picture and points out the soft-spoken István Pálos. The long face is the same, but I would not have recognised him without his full beard. Vili Schmidt, their friend who led the Budafok group against the Russians, is sitting in the front row. His face and rough clothes are smeared with dirt, and I remember Pálos telling me that Vili was always *piszkos* – grubby. But the most striking thing about him is how young he seems. How young they all are, barely more than teenagers.

Suzanne bends over the photograph again. She points to a young man on her right.

'That's my brother.'

Suzanne's brother left Hungary two days before her and László, and they met up again in Vienna. He had also recently got engaged, to a girl called Giza. He had expected Giza to come out with the Budaházys when they left. Suzanne and László had tried to persuade her, but she refused to go. When Suzanne's brother heard that Giza was still in Hungary, he was devastated. He stayed in Vienna just long enough to see Suzanne married. Then, just before Christmas, he went back for his fiancée.

'They wanted to come out in the New Year's night,' Suzanne says. 'Because everybody celebrated, everybody so busy with something else.'

But her brother would not be so lucky, second time around. The borders had tightened, and the flow of refugees had slowed to a trickle. The young couple made it as far as the border, but then they were caught and sent back to Budapest.

'And for one year,' Suzanne says, 'they was perfectly all right. He was working, his fiancée was working.'

'For one year,' her husband cuts in, 'the Communists wasn't sure of anything. They couldn't push the Hungarians as hard. They didn't mess about with little fish like my brother-in-law – all he did, he drove a couple of trucks for us with weapons. They let them lay down. They thought that once we catch the big fish, then we start on the little fish. And that's when they got to Budafok.

'They took four or five people who were in there. Dr Takács, he was a well-loved doctor, he was in charge of the hospital. And another guy, who was a building contractor, Pongrátz Bácsi.'

And Suzanne's brother.

At her brother's trial, the man who testified against him was police lieutenant Ersai. The same lieutenant Ersai who lost his fingers through spying – the man whose life László Budaházy once chose to spare. Ersai picked Suzanne's brother out as one of the Budafok gang. Because of that, he was sentenced to seven years in the hard labour prison of Recsk.

Their mother died while he was still in jail. The family home lay empty, and the Communists seized it.

'When her brother came out from the jail, there was a new house where their house was. Just like that. And when he asked: "What's this house here?" They said, "You shut up – or you wanna go back where you come from?"'

Now, when Budaházy thinks of the day he met Ersai in Budafok's Town Square, he regrets the decision he made, the compassion that he felt.

'I should have shot him just the same.'

Budaházy passes me some more photographs. In colour, they were taken just a few years ago. It is winter. The Town Hall of Budafok, with its steep roofs and baroque turrets, is blanketed in snow. Before it, on a mound of earth in white parklands, stands a monument made of roughly hewn stone. The front bears the legend: '1956'. On the back, in two columns, are engraved the names of the dead. Thirteen who died during the fighting; nine who were executed afterwards. Gyula (Öcsi) Schäffer – the young man shot in the head on the second day of the uprising – is one of them. The statue of a weeping woman stands guard over the monument, tall and black against the snow.

A friend of the Budaházys took the photographs, and sent them to Australia. László and Suzanne have not seen the monument for themselves. They have never been back to Hungary since escaping over the border. Not even once.

'I never got amnesty!' Budaházy declares, when I express my surprise. 'Because I was classified as a murdering hooligan!'

A few months after they left Hungary, a friend sent them a copy of *Esti Budapest*, the evening newspaper. It carried a photograph of Öcsi Schäffer's funeral.

The article was headed: 'Vili Schmidt and his band of hooligans'. In the photograph, the young men of Budafok were standing around with machine guns raised. They had fired them into the air in a farewell salute.

'We gave him a big send off,' Budaházy says. 'We buried him like a soldier.'

The women were standing guard around the head of the coffin. Suzanne was among them. Someone had drawn a circle around her face.

'Nobody's face was straight on,' László says. 'But her face you could recognise straight away.'

Neither of them remembers seeing anyone with a camera that day.

'I would have killed him!' László exclaims.

'They were looking for me,' Suzanne says. 'That's why I couldn't go back. Both of us was guilty, to them.'

Even in the late 1960s, when the amnesty was announced, there was still a list of 5,000 people who were viewed as killers. Budaházy discovered that both his and Vili Schmidt's names were on that list. The amnesty didn't apply to them.

'We wouldn't get a visa. And if we get a visa somehow, and we get caught – they have to start proceedings.'

'That's why when my mum was sick,' Suzanne says, 'I couldn't go home.'

She hadn't realised, when she left Budapest, that she would never see her mother again. Hadn't guessed that she wouldn't even be able to attend her funeral.

László shrugs. 'That was the price we had to pay.'

Vili Schmidt had come across to Australia on the same forty-two day sea journey as the Budaházys. He also settled in Melbourne. He married an English woman, and separated himself completely from the local Hungarians.

'Sometimes we get together,' Budaházy says, 'and he looks after the words, he can't find them. After about an hour, he gets back to Hungarian. But he never use it! He never mix with any Hungarians. His father was one of the Revolutionary Council's elected representatives; but the elite of the Hungarian community here never recognised us for what we were.'

'He is living in Essendon,' Suzanne says. 'He will never be back. He'll never be back.'

And what about the Budaházys – now that things have changed in Hungary, would they ever consider returning?

'We are too old to travel,' Suzanne says. 'Australia is a good country, give us a good living. But it's very hard to say we are not Hungarians; and very hard to say we are not Australians.'

They have reached a point of balance in themselves, between the old country they brought with them, and the new country they have made their own.

There is one more thing that Budaházy wants to show me. Beside the photographs on the kitchen bench there is a cardboard tube. Budaházy slides a piece of stiff paper from the tube, and spreads it flat. It is a certificate, the words are in Hungarian.

'From out of the blue, I got this scroll from the Parliament of Budapest, which recognised what you did in the revolution.'

Yet it will never hang framed on his wall.

'Another people who is came out in 1948,' Suzanne explains, 'and then went back to visit Hungary – they got recognised as a 1956 fighter. He came back and he was laughing his head off! He said, "Look, I got this, and I was not even in Hungary!"'

'I know another one,' Budaházy adds, 'who never even been in Hungary. He lived in Yugoslavia. The first time he ever saw Hungary was maybe five, ten years ago. And he got a recognition for 1956! I don't want to tell you the name, but I know who he is.

'And that's why I don't want this. I don't want anything. Because if these people can get it, why should I?'

His voice is strong with pride. Budaházy would never go looking for honours, but I can hear the hurt in his words. He believes that this almost random issuing of certificates devalues what he went through.

Budaházy rolls up his certificate, and slips it into the cardboard tube it was mailed in. Supporting himself on his cane, he carries the tube to the far end of the kitchen and puts it in the cupboard with the photographs. His movements have a firm decisiveness to them. He will never go back to Hungary. There is a sense of finality as he closes the door.

IT WAS THE last few days of November, 1956. In Budafok, Vilmos Schmidt senior had returned from the latest Council meeting with the news that it was all over. Across the river, the resistance fighters of Csepel had finally fallen silent.

István Pálos still had his weapons – a Russian machine pistol, hand grenades and a rifle. He wrapped them in layers of newspaper greased with sump oil. Then he looked for a place to hide them. There were six steps up to the ground floor of his family house, with a basement beneath the stairs. Pálos opened up a hole in the brickwork, and placed his wrapped weapons in a small recess beneath one of the large flagstone steps.

Then, early in the morning, Pálos left his home and headed for the train station in Kelenföld. Even Pálos's father, who had already lost one son, agreed that it was too risky for him to stay.

Pálos was wearing woollen trousers and a jumper, as protection against the cold. Over this he pulled on a stiff leather jacket that he had bought at a second hand market. He also had a pair of ex-Army boots. They were full leather – unlike the regular issue soldiers' boots, which were made partly from waxed canvas. They reached to just below his calf.

'Someone had put holes down the side, with a leather thong,' Pálos says. He is sitting in my living room, a mug of cooling coffee and a plate of biscuits beside him. 'So you could lace it up. And I wore it with the top three inches folded back, over these leather thongs. It was very fashionable, I was very proud of it. It was very heavy – now I couldn't imagine how could you walk. You got used to it.'

He had a sandwich in one pocket of his jacket. In the other was a fresh pair of socks. Apart from some money, Pálos took nothing else. He was travelling with several other people from the district, including a family with two young children – a brother and sister, five and seven years old. There were around ten of them altogether. They arrived at the train station just after dawn and bought tickets that would take them west, almost to the border.

'The train was absolutely packed. Full house. We started off, and then the conductor come. He never checked the tickets. Just wished everybody good luck.'

The train journey lasted through the morning and well into the afternoon. Eventually they reached a village, a few stops before the main western town of Sopron. Not wanting to risk going all the way into town, Pálos and his companions jumped off.

The village was so small that there was not even a station. No one in the group had brought a map, so they had very little idea where they were, or how to get to Austria. All they could see were fields, stretching away flat on either side. It was a bright afternoon, and the sun was just beginning to sink towards the western horizon. The group took their bearings from it. They started walking.

The crops had been harvested from the fields, and the ground was freshly turned. Most of the other people on the train had jumped off as well. Everyone was heading in the same direction.

'To the horizon, there was people walking.'

Pálos's group trudged on across the ploughed fields. The two children kept up as best they could. They walked for a long time. The sun fell below the horizon. As the light faded it grew cold and damp. There was no moon; but the sky was clear and stars sparkled in the darkness above them.

From ahead came the sporadic sound of shooting, which confirmed they were drawing closer to the border. Every now and then, a flare would streak noisily into the sky, illuminating the night. Pálos estimated the border was only another kilometre or two away, but by this time the five-year-old was struggling. Pálos lifted the boy onto his shoulders and they kept going.

'And then we saw some lights – houses. We came down on a kind of track. We were all together again. Sometimes we gathered people; sometimes we missed out on people. But this nucleus of ten of us managed to stay together.'

One of their group went ahead into the village, to see what he could find out. The rest of them waited in the dark. When their friend returned, he had good news. There was a man who would help them across the border, and they could wait inside his house.

They proceeded into the village, and went to the house. The owner invited them into the warmth. He offered them something hot to drink, and Pálos and his friends gratefully accepted. To their surprise, they found another fifteen people already crowded into the room. All of them were expecting to cross the border that night.

'You have to wait until a bit later to get across,' the householder told them. 'Now, how much money you have?'

He went around the room, collecting money from each person in turn. Most people had two or three hundred forints to offer.

'And that was the first real disappointment,' Pálos says.

Until then, the people he had come across had been more than willing to help without any thought of reward. For Pálos, it was the most wonderful and extraordinary aspect of the uprising – that the whole country was united behind a common cause. Now, for the first time, Pálos had encountered someone who was out for personal gain. It hurt him much more than the loss of a little money.

'I chipped in two hundred, but I had about a thousand on me. And he said: "No more? That's not enough – no more?" Later on, I was talking to some people outside [Hungary], and they said, "Oh, you were lucky! They were not really scalpers." Because they went to a different village, and they even had to give their wedding ring.'

Pálos waited with the others in the house. Around midnight, the householder said: 'All right – let's go!' Everyone followed him outside. They started off across the fields, and after a few kilometres they reached a ditch. Bushes covered its steep sides. After they had scrambled across the ditch, the householder told them: 'This is the border. *Viszontlátásra* – goodbye! That is Austria.'

They did not have to walk much further before they saw lights. It was a small farm. Austrians were waiting for them, with food ready. There was a tractor with a large trailer that was half-filled with straw. They climbed into the trailer and were taken to a Red Cross station nearby.

'The little girl was a bit tired. She was a bit of a plumpish girl. And the boy was tired, but not really crying, not complaining – the boy never complained.'

Pálos spent the rest of the night at the Red Cross centre. He could have stayed longer, but he had an address in Vienna to reach. It was where all the Budafok youth had agreed to meet up again, if they made it across the border.

So first thing the following morning, Pálos left the Red Cross with some of his friends, intending to hitchhike into Vienna. It wasn't long before a truck stopped for them. The weather had turned suddenly icy, and when they climbed in the back they found the truck's load had frosted over.

'Luckily, because they were carting manure! It was absolutely awful, but it didn't coat us because it was frozen already.'

Pálos reached his address in Vienna. As other people from Budafok arrived, they also did the same, and before long, the entire group was together again. Their leader, Vili Schmidt junior, made it out with his parents; the Budaházys, László and Suzanne, held their wedding there. Food was provided at the refugee centres where they were billeted, and transport around Vienna was free. As well as this, they received thirty schillings a fortnight to spend as they wished.

'We bought chocolate.' Pálos is a man after my own heart. 'The cheapest chocolate was the cooking chocolate. So – a kilo of cooking chocolate, three or four oranges, and sit in the movie.'

Pálos hadn't eaten an orange since he was five years old. They sat in the movie theatre as the snow fell outside, watching the western films that were all banned in Hungary. The Lone Ranger was popular at the time.

'And we registered to everywhere – America, Australia … They always said: "Sorry, you can register, but nothing in the near future." And Australia called us first.'

My black cat, Molly, has come into the room. She pads carefully across the map of Budapest that is laid out on the floor, the paper crinkling under her paws. Then she rubs herself against Pálos's legs, considering whether to jump into his lap. Pálos does his best to ignore her. I try to coax her towards me instead. There are a few more questions I want to ask Pálos, before he leaves tonight.

'I never, ever felt really homesick,' he says, in response to one of these. 'You know why? Because I had to come. People who make their choice, they can't find their place. Many go back, come out again, go back and see their families. Then after a few years they are disappointed and come out again.'

This pulls me up, makes me think. As soon as there is choice, there is indecision. There is the dark possibility of regret. I am a citizen of both England and Australia. My father is Hungarian – I could take his nationality as well. But two is already more than enough.

When I was a child, the world was small, and home was easy to identify. It was a pink bedroom, a cream carpet with synthetic pile.

It was the pink roses on the wallpaper that my father hung himself, taking great care to match the repeating pattern. At night in bed, waiting to fall asleep, I would run my fingers over the bubbles beneath the rose-covered paper, pushing the trapped air sideways, trying to set it free.

Now things are different, more complex. I have lived in three separate countries and feel a connection with them all. I have felt the ache, the constant wondering: have I done the right thing? It is a yearning for home, when home is not to be found in a single physical place any more.

'From the beginning, we were hoping to get back somehow,' Pálos continues, following a train of thought that seems to partly contradict what he has just said. 'But as soon as you settle down, get married and have kids, that was absolutely out of the question.'

He has been back to Hungary only once, in 1975.

'It was the first and last time,' he says.

His brother and father were still living in the same house in Budafok, but it was about to be demolished to make way for tower block apartments. Pálos was worried about the weapons he had left behind in 1956, hidden beneath the steps of the old house. When the land was redeveloped, the builders would discover them. His family might get into trouble.

Pálos hired a combi van and drove into Hungary through Germany and Austria. He arrived on the outskirts of Budapest as darkness fell. Driving through the streets of Budafok, everything seemed much smaller than in his memories. Yet it still felt like coming home. His father had prepared a huge spread of food to welcome him, but all that Pálos ate were slices of fresh Hungarian bread. He couldn't get enough of it. The taste was rich and familiar, redolent of his schooldays – so different from the bread in Melbourne.

Pálos retrieved the machine pistol from under the house steps and sawed it in half. He put the pieces in a bag with the hand grenades. Then he took the bag down to the bank of the Danube. He hadn't expected to find people strolling up and down and, at first, he couldn't find a secluded spot. He began to grow anxious. But then there was a quieter moment. He seized his chance, and hurled the equipment into the river.

Only one gun remained: a Russian-style carbine. Pálos didn't have the heart to destroy it. Instead, he dismantled it. He placed the pieces in the lining of his hired combi van, together with seventeen rounds of ammunition. When the time came to leave, he drove the van back to Austria.

'In the border they asking about pictures of great value,' Pálos laughs, 'and how much salami you taking – that sort of thing. They never thought somebody taking guns out!'

He still has the carbine, and has put it on display from time to time. The end of the barrel and a few of the other parts are a little rusty, although overall the sump oil did its job. But when Pálos retrieved the gun from under the steps, in a way it was the end of his hopes for his country. At the time he hid his weapons, all those years ago, he was thinking that either he would come back to use them himself one day; or that others would need them when they took up the fight.

But there was never to be another uprising. Young people had fled the country in droves. Many of those who stayed behind were executed or imprisoned. The Communists knew there were large numbers of weapons still out in the community, and they were on their guard.

It would be another thirty-three years before Hungary was finally free. And this time, it would be a revolution without violence.

Meanwhile, in Australia, Pálos channelled his passion for his homeland into his involvement with the Hungarian community. He devoted much of his time to forming and leading a scout group for the children of migrants. It became a kind of mission for him to ensure that the language and culture would live on into future generations. For Pálos, it was a way to continue what the fighting had been about.

When 1989 came, Pálos was as surprised as anyone. It was not that he had given up hope, but he had resigned himself to the Communists staying for a long time. After all, the Turkish occupation of Hungary – in the 17th and 18th centuries – had lasted more than 150 years. So when Pálos watched the news bulletins of the last Russian soldiers leaving Hungary, he felt great excitement. Even so, he knew it had come too late for him to return. He had made a new life in Australia, he felt settled.

And emotionally, he had never really left his homeland behind.

'There are beautiful books about people leaving after the War,' Pálos says thoughtfully, as my cat Molly rubs against his legs. 'Some of them had a handful of soil. Some of them, in beautiful lighting in the last town, turned back and looked at the country. I never turned back, I never looked back. I never had a piece of soil. Because you don't need physical things for what is in your heart.'

A WINDING concrete path takes me across flat green lawns, following the course of the Danube. On this unseasonably warm afternoon there are joggers, and people out walking their dogs. Across the river rise the smoke stacks of Csepel. A few metres below the path, at the water's edge, there is a thin strip of gravelly beach. It is deserted. There doesn't seem to be any way to reach it, other than sliding down a steep, grassy embankment. Somewhere along here, the 'Golden Youth' of Budafok used to gather. This is where Suzanne and László Budaházy first met.

My own parents met in Abbey Park, a quiet, tidy English park, among the perfumed hedges and expansive green lawns. The town was Leicester, at the centre of England, known best for its market and its clock tower. Pat, my mother, had always lived there. My father had gone there for the work.

One Sunday in late July, seventeen-year-old Pat, a clerk at the County Court, was sitting on a bench with her friend Valerie. The park was where young people congregated on Sundays, it was the place to meet friends and be seen. The large-headed summer roses would be perfect for two or three weeks more, before the petals began to fall. The two girls were wearing their good dresses – it was warm enough to go without cardigans – and their hair was teased high on their heads.

Péter was strolling the paths with his old friend Öcsi Fodor. The two men had stayed together, after escaping Hungary almost four years before. The motorcycle accident that would take Öcsi's leg

237

was still in the future. Things were going well for Péter. He had just changed jobs: from the night shift at a hosiery factory, to day work with General Electric. He had his Austin Metropolitan sports car, which he had bought when he came out of the Merchant Navy. He and Öcsi were satisfied with their new lives, full of confidence. When they noticed the two English girls sitting on their bench, they wandered across to talk to them.

Öcsi and Valerie did not take to each other. But Péter had an advantage with Pat – he had a talent for cooking, and Pat was constantly hungry. She would visit him at his lodgings on Howard Road, and eat the food he prepared – hot salami and spicy sausages from the local Polish butcher, *paprikás*, *gulyás* soup.

Pat's mother objected to the relationship. Her high expectations for her daughter didn't include marrying a foreigner, especially not a Hungarian refugee. She was the grand matriarch of the home, her husband and son quietly acquiescent, preferring an uneasy peace over conflict. But Pat was stubborn, strong-willed, more than a match for her mother. She refused to stop seeing Péter, and their relationship flourished.

Eventually, one evening, Pat's mother threw her out of the family home. Pat was tired of the continual fights anyway, the arguments repeating like circular tape. She snatched her pushbike and cycled over to Howard Road. Once there, she knocked on the glass of Péter's window until he let her in. His Polish landlady put cushions out in the kitchen for Péter to sleep on, and Pat spent the night in his bed. Next morning, she went out and found lodgings of her own. In a self-imposed exile of her own, she never went home again.

My mother and father were married on St Patrick's Day 1962, at the Registry Office on Paddington's Walk. Öcsi was best man. The bride wore green – a bouclé tweed suit with a Peter Pan collar, and a black bow of Persian lambs wool. Péter's dark blue suit was custom-made from thick, durable fabric, with his name sewn into the pocket.

'I still have that suit,' he tells me. 'And it still fits me. I'm going to be buried in it!'

Pat sent her mother an invitation, but received no response. Then, on the day of the marriage, one of the guests noticed a woman outside behaving strangely.

'She was saying she'd come to see a wedding,' the guest told Pat. 'But she isn't here … you know, I think it must be your mother!'

When Pat and Péter left the Registry Office, Pat's mother was on the other side of the road with Pat's nine-year-old brother, Edward. As soon as the couple emerged, Pat's mother ducked behind a parked car, pulling Edward down with her. Péter's Austin Metropolitan was not far from where she was hiding. The couple had no choice but to walk towards her. As they drew closer, my grandmother quickly stood and scuttled away down the street, dragging young Edward after her.

Pat and Péter didn't try to follow. They went back instead to Howard Road, where the Polish landlady had prepared their reception. The food was washed down with glasses of strong cherry vodka.

My grandmother reappeared for a while when my brother and I were born, but when we grew beyond babies, she vanished again. I never got to know her and my grandfather, or my uncle Edward. There were always just the four of us – my parents, my brother and me; my Hungarian relatives too distant to be thought of as real family. A narrow sense of home.

In Budafok, traffic roars along the highway leading into the centre of Budapest. Turning away from the river I walk through an underpass, the concrete walls bright and solid with graffiti. It brings me out into the main square. The Town Hall is on the left, an ornate building of yellow walls with a red-tiled roof. A juliet balcony juts beneath a row of gothic windows, and two white turrets frame the façade. Directly opposite the Town Hall, on the other side of the square, is the local police headquarters. More utilitarian, a tall radio antenna decorates the roof, and a squat air-conditioning unit hangs like a wart beneath one of the plain windows. In between the two buildings lie pretty, landscaped gardens.

Then I see it. A small, grassy mound, rising from a patch of lawn. At the top, a block of roughly hewn stone. The back of the monument is towards me – the pale stone sheared flat, with two separate lists: the names of the dead. Except for the lack of snow, this is László Budaházy's photograph.

I walk around to the front. Ten steps lead up to where the dark woman stands with her head in her hands, a long shawl draped over her body. Beside her, in dark, flowing script on the monument's face, there is just a year: '1956'. The tails of the first three numbers stream down the rough stone.

A note tells me it was built in 2001. After forty years of silence, this is the acknowledgement that Budaházy is unlikely ever to see for himself. His children, busy with lives and families of their own, have never visited Hungary; but perhaps one day they will. Or perhaps their children will. And when they come, the monument will be here for them to find.

I have made my own journey back, and have found the past reflected in the museum displays, and the monuments to 1956. Witch-hunts and purges have so far been avoided. There are those who believe that a delayed accounting is still to come, but I'm not so sure. As the years add distance, I suspect the old Communists will have nothing but their own restless thoughts to disturb their sleep at night.

As I wander around the city, the monuments seem to be everywhere. There is the plump boy insurgent on guard outside the Corvin Cinema. An eternal flame burns in front of Parliament House. Even the glossy Mammut shopping mall in Buda has a display of carved burial posts strung with tricolour ribbons, beside a rippling flag of silver metal. Young people sit, posturing and smoking, on the wide entrance steps to the mall. It has become their meeting place – more appealing than the park, the beach or the local coffee shop. The building's blind, reflective sides tower above them, overshadowing Széna tér.

On the other side of the city, mature trees flank the wide paths of Kerepesi cemetery. Leaves and shiny horse chestnuts are scattered across the uneven ground, among the old gravestones. The traffic of busy Fiumei út is muted, and the rumble of trains heading eastwards from Keleti station barely makes it over the high concrete walls. It is an oasis of calm.

The proliferation of monuments throughout the city has left me untouched. I feel strangely distanced, even weary. I am starting to see it as nothing more than political point scoring. Perhaps I am succumbing to Hungarian cynicism, a healthy national trait. But I am filled with a yearning for the individual, the personal; I want to feel a sense of connection with history and with family. This is probably what I've been searching for all along – the elements of a sense of home. Although I am gradually realising I'll be unlikely to find that here, in a country where I will always be an outsider. Still, I hope to come closer to it within the peace of Kerepesi's walls.

Beside one of the wide avenues lies the grave of János Kádár. He was the Communist leader complicit in the suppression of the uprising, as well as the executions of László Rajk and Imre Nagy. Kádár's tomb, made from large blocks of red granite, has his name and the dates engraved in gold. That's all – he needs no explanation. There are fresh flowers, red, green and white, on

241

either side of the headstone. Some view him as a man who betrayed his country, but it seems there are still those who want to keep his memory alive.

At the end of his life, Kádár was in ill health, and under pressure from his Party colleagues to move aside. He clung to power, even though he could find no answer to Hungary's urgent economic problems and spiralling foreign currency debt. His uncanny political astuteness – which had allowed him to survive so well for so long – failed him at the end. He was losing his grip, and in May 1988 he had no choice but to resign.

By the beginning of the following year, the re-evaluation of Hungary's Communist history had begun. There were significant shifts in thinking – 1956 was finally acknowledged as a 'popular uprising' rather than a 'counter-revolution'. In April that year, in what would turn out to be Kádár's last speech to the Party Central Committee, his words even suggested regret for some of the things he had done.

'From a distance of thirty years,' he said, 'I am sorry for everybody.'

Two months later, Imre Nagy was given a ceremonial reburial in Budapest. A quarter of a million people crowded into Heroes' Square that day, and many more eagerly followed the event on television. Kádár lived just long enough to see it. He died three weeks later, at the age of 77 – confused, but unswayed in his belief in the socialist cause.

It was an eventful year. That autumn, Hungary opened its border with Austria. Thousands of East Germans flooded across it into the West. It was the beginning of the end. It was probably fortunate for Kádár that he did not live to see the Berlin Wall come down.

Further along the tree-lined cemetery avenue, on the opposite side of the pathway to Kádár's grave, there is a large area of dry, patchy grass. Clinging to its far edge is a small cluster of graves, all relatively recent. They are arranged in neat rows, most with a simple black crucifix perched on a mound of turned earth. A few can be no more than a couple of days old: the fresh soil still holds the mark of footprints, and they are heaped with wreaths and ribbons in the ubiquitous red, white and green. One streamer bears the words: 'We are proud of you'. Red roses, their petals intact, hang their limp heads.

This is the plot set aside for the Fifty-sixers, the men and women who fought in the uprising. For thirty years they were outsiders, shunned by the régime, but now they have their own place. As they die, they will be buried here.

Wandering among the simple graves, reading the names, I realise I have found what I was looking for. No longer just symbols, these are real people to me. I have heard enough stories now to be able to imagine these other lives. The ghosts walk with me, close enough to touch. I can feel them as if they were still alive.

Beyond the last of the crucifixes, the flat, hard ground stretches away towards the cemetery entrance. The patchy grass can take many more graves. Communists and revolutionaries, both commemorated at Kerepesi. Because we all end up in the same place. After a beautiful day, the autumn air has turned crisp and refreshing, it has a different taste and smell from Australian air. I look across the cemetery and think of the Budaházys again, and how they will never return to the soil of their home.

My last full day in Budapest is the only day of rain. It begins in the morning with showers, and by mid-afternoon the rain is falling steadily. The city is veiled in sheets of grey silk. Muted and slow, melancholic, the day drifts towards dusk.

I have heard enough stories for the city to be transformed. The ghosts roam further than the calm avenues of the cemetery – they are everywhere I look now, in the streets and parks of Budapest. They are the echoes of the living, as well as the dead.

In the Museum gardens, the ghost of Sándor Tóth crawls on his belly across the landscaped grounds. Late in the day, I watch him take shelter behind a slender statue in the gathering dusk. At the back of the Museum, beyond a dense knot of parked cars, the ghosts of ÁVO officers fire tracer bullets through white wrought iron bars. And at the Károlyi gardens, locked in for the night behind tall gates, the ghost of young Márta Németh – János Dabasy's favourite niece – wanders the winding paths.

Back in Mr Horváth's apartment, the ceiling above the window springs a leak. At first, the flow is gentle enough to contain in a cup. But a few minutes later, first one heavy stream and then another breaks out, thudding onto the parquet floor. I run to fetch tin saucepans from the kitchen. The collection of pans grows as the water finds new points of weakness to trickle through. For the first time, I see that the white paint on that section of the ceiling is already blistered and brown-stained, from when it has rained before.

'It should have been fixed,' Tibor says when I call to let him know. 'I'll send someone around tomorrow afternoon.'

I will be gone by then, enduring the long plane journey to Australia.

I stand at the window. The drumming water beats out an atonal rhythm behind me, rising in pitch as the saucepans fill. Rain inside and out. Across the street, at the Intercontinental Hotel, the lamps are lit in several of the rooms. Each room has the same contemporary lamp, standing on the same stained wood table, directly in front of the net-curtained window. Only the shadowy figures beyond each light are different, moving about in their temporary homes. I try to imagine their lives, what has brought them to Budapest.

From the apartment on the floor above mine comes the sound of footsteps, the gentle murmur of voices. The persistent drip of water into the saucepans has slowed, and grown soothing. I am here, and

244

at the same time not-here, already thinking of my other home. Already longing for the different isolation of Melbourne's flat picket-fence suburbs, radiating endlessly out from the tall, tight nucleus of the city.

I empty the saucepans into the kitchen sink, and replace them under the drips. That will hold it for a few hours, I think. Then I lock István Horváth's door behind me for almost the last time. His nameplate gleams in the dim balcony light, asserting ownership – the apartment has always been his home, not mine. This has always been his country, and can never be mine. I have simply occupied them both for a short while.

It is a brief walk through the drizzle, past the Intercontinental, to the river embankment. The white lights of a restaurant ship reflect from the water. I feel wide awake at last, my jet lag finally gone. Stepping carefully over the sloping wooden gangplank, I slip out of the grey, lethargic day.

The restaurant is bathed in eternal summer, all white tablecloths and blond wood. Martin and his girlfriend, Viki, are waiting for me. The food is Asian-influenced, delicately flavoured and beautifully presented. It's the kind of meal you'd expect to find in London or Paris, with prices to match. But the people around us are not speaking English, French or even German. They are mostly Hungarians, and mostly quite young. I am reminded how far Budapest has come.

'You've been here a long time now,' I say to Martin. One of the few expatriates who have stayed on, he is part of a dying breed. 'Don't you miss New Zealand? Aren't you thinking about going home?'

'Yes – I've been thinking about it.' He shrugs. 'I won't be going back next year. But maybe the one after that.'

I tell them what István Pálos said about migration – that those who change countries through choice cannot find their place.

'They bounce backwards and forwards, always feeling that they're missing something, that they might be happier in the other place. People who don't have a choice settle more easily. Because they're resigned to it, they make the best of things.'

Martin and Viki are no longer looking at me. They are staring intently at each other instead. I shut up.

'You don't have any choice,' Martin tells Viki at last. 'So it'll be fine.'

His tone is light, but it's clear he understands the magnitude of what he is asking: the hardship of living in exile. Viki says nothing. But her dark, expressive eyes widen, and she gives a small shrug. I have already said too much, so I decide not to tell them what the pastor János Dabasy seemed to believe – that exile is always a choice, and there is always a yearning for home.

Through the restaurant windows, lights sparkle on the Danube's softly flowing water. The Chain Bridge and the fairytale castle on the hill are floodlit, molten gold against the dark, damp sky. It is hard to leave this magical city, but I am lucky to have a choice. I can always come back, if I need to. Choice simply means that it takes longer to find yourself, that's all.

When I board the plane for Melbourne in the morning, my stomach already sinking with a sense of loss, I will try to remember that. And I will remind myself of something else that István Pálos said: you don't need physical things for what is in your heart.

THE RED letter sits on my desk, waiting for me. Each time I read it, the language gets a little easier. The sentences become more ready to yield up meaning, the expressions are less obscure. Even so, I have transcribed the letter into English – my mother's tongue. In translation, I can find the pieces of the story more easily. I can turn quickly to a particular phrase or word. I pick it up now and leaf through to the final section. The place where it all ends and begins.

Péter Mándoki and Öcsi Fodor stood outside Budapest's Keleti station, at the foot of the broad entrance steps. It was Christmas Day, 1956, and they had just arrived. The tall buildings around them were indistinct, fogged by a mist of fine snow. It was early evening, and already quite dark. The departure point for trains to the border was across the city, at Déli station, but no trams were running. The men had never been to Budapest before, and they had no idea how to reach the station on foot.

As they hesitated, a motorcyclist appeared out of the mist and drew up beside them. The bike had a sidecar attached.

'Where do you want to go?' the rider asked.

'Will you take us to Déli? How much will it cost?'

They agreed on a price. Öcsi climbed up behind the rider, while Péter settled into the sidecar.

'We can't go by the main routes,' the cyclist warned. 'There are tanks on every road.'

They sped through the narrow side streets, turning left and right so frequently that Péter soon became disoriented. From the sidecar he could see very little. The snow was still falling. The motorbike jolted across the cobblestones. Déli was on the other side of the Danube, but Péter couldn't even tell whether they had crossed the river yet. He and Öcsi had to submit completely to the volition of the motorcyclist. There wasn't any choice.

The bike finally came to a stop. They were in a small street not far from Déli station, and the cyclist showed them which way to go. Then he sped away.

Péter and Öcsi found the station largely deserted. There were no queues at the cashier's window. Péter bought two tickets to Szombathely, a town close to the Austrian border.

'How long will it be to the next train?'

The cashier shrugged. 'I can't tell you.'

In the quiet, empty waiting room, Péter and Öcsi sat and watched the hours drift past. Gradually a group of people, most of them young, began to gather in the darkness outside. They stood in complete silence, smoking, or with hands buried deep in their pockets. No one wanted to risk talking to anyone else.

It was after eleven that night when the Szombathely train was finally announced. Péter and Öcsi were relieved. It might have been their first visit to the capital, but all they wanted to do was leave Budapest far behind. They found an empty compartment and took it, not yet daring to put their trust in strangers. As the train pulled away from the city they took out the food they had brought with them from Horváti. Péter stared at it.

'I don't have the appetite for this,' he said.

Even the wine failed to go down easily – their demijohns still held a good few litres of the golden liquid that tasted of home.

The train rattled on through the night. Fields flashed past in the blackness, plains of snow glittering under moonlight. Péter and Öcsi were in no mood for sleep. They feared that they would be challenged at any moment and be required to show their identity cards; but dawn broke, and no one had come to disturb them. The

248

train continued slowly on, with long pauses at small stations, a string of names that Péter and Öcsi didn't recognise.

Close to midday, the door of their compartment was pushed open. The ticket collector leaned in.

'We're coming up to the last station,' the collector told them. 'The train will slow down before it reaches the town. Whoever doesn't have the right papers should jump off there – the station is full of Russian soldiers.'

He snapped the door shut, and Péter heard him continue on along the corridor. The two friends stepped outside and made their way to the end of the carriage. Soon afterwards, they heard the engine's brakes grind on, and the train slowed to a crawl. Peering through the window, Péter saw rows of snow-covered pines. He and Öcsi opened the door and jumped to the ground. Glancing back, Péter saw hundreds of people leaping from both sides of the slowly moving train. They ran from the tracks, and disappeared into the trees.

Péter and Öcsi also headed for the safety of the forest. Among the frosty pines they ran into a group of three young men, roughly their own age. The three strangers were wandering aimlessly.

'We don't know this area,' one of them said.

'What will happen if you do find the border?' Péter asked. 'Do you know how you'll get across?'

The man shrugged. 'We don't have any plans. We thought we would work it out when we got there.'

Péter and Öcsi showed the men the address they had – a house in a village called Disznoshorváti. There was someone there who could help them. But first, they needed to find the village. All they knew was that it was close to Szombathely, and they could not be too far away.

Öcsi and the others looked to Péter for guidance. At twenty-three, he was the oldest in the group, but the responsibility weighed heavily on him. He decided to lead them a little further into the woods for safety, while taking care not to go so deep that they would lose all sense of direction.

It was a young forest. Many of the pines were saplings, the trunks no more than twenty centimetres thick. There were often wide spaces between the trees. The men trudged uphill through deep snow. From higher ground, they thought they might be able to see where they should go. From time to time they stopped to consult in whispers. Even the gentlest of sounds carried long distances in the frosty air.

It was growing late, and the light was fading. The harsh barking of dogs drifted towards them across the forest. The approaching darkness made Péter anxious, although he kept his concerns from the others – he worried they might become lost on the hill, and have to spend the night out in the open. Displaying a confidence he did not feel, he led the group in the direction of the barking dogs. He hoped to find houses there, at the edge of the forest.

Suddenly, through the thinning trees, they noticed ribbons of smoke winding into the air. They had come out high on the hillside. Directly below them lay a village, the houses built into the lower slopes. Smoke was rising from the chimneys.

The five men edged their way down the hill. When they were close to the village, they stopped to rest.

'We should stay hidden here, among the trees,' Péter cautioned, 'while there's still light in the sky.'

They hunkered down and waited. No sound came from the houses. When it was completely dark, they emerged cautiously from the woods and scrambled down the hillside into the village. Péter checked the name of the first street that they came to. No one was more surprised than him to find it was the one mentioned in his directions. They were in Disznoshorváti – by sheer luck, they had stumbled across the very place they had been searching for.

The boys knocked at the third house in the street. A short, middle-aged man with grey hair opened the door. When Péter explained who they were, the man pulled them quickly inside and had them sit by the fire. It was a relief to escape the cold.

The grey-haired man's first question was: 'Do you have a little good wine?'

He still remembered the wine that Péter's neighbours had brought with them several weeks earlier, imbued with the sweetness of grapes cultivated on Erdőhorváti's fertile hills. He was eager to taste it again.

The demijohns were brought out and passed around the room. Péter was the only one who could not bring himself to drink. Their journey was not yet over. He would not be able to relax until it was.

There was very little wine left when their host finally stood up.

'I'm going out now. I'll find the guide who'll take you across the border.'

But when the man returned a short time later, he was alone. From his face, Péter could see he had bad news.

'The man who was going to guide you left the village last night with a group of refugees,' the grey-haired man said. 'He isn't back yet. No one knows if he's been caught; or if he's still out in the open somewhere. He might be trying to make his way back. All I can tell you is, you can't stay here for long – Russian soldiers are always coming through, searching for people.'

Péter thought desperately. They wouldn't get another guide now – they had left their escape too late. It was too risky for anyone else to try and help them.

He turned to the others. 'As far as I can see,' he said, 'we've got two choices. Either we go forwards without a guide; or we turn around and go back the way we came.'

They were all in agreement.

'We've come too far to turn back now.'

The five of them waited at the house until ten in the evening. Their host stepped outside to check that the coast was clear. When he gave the signal, they all followed him out into the village. He took them as far as the edge of the houses.

'Austria is over there.' He pointed across white fields, the snow luminous under the moon. 'It's only five kilometres to the border, but you need to be careful – Russian soldiers are always patrolling there.'

As before, Öcsi and the others looked to Péter for their lead. He noticed that one of the fields had a line of bare fruit trees. The line ran in the direction they needed to take.

'Those will give us a bit of cover,' he said. 'It's better than nothing.'

They headed out across the field in single file. Péter was at the front, moving cautiously from tree to tree. Suddenly he heard a sound ahead. He hit the snow, face down. Behind him, the others did the same. Péter watched as two soldiers strolled along the far end of the field. The soldiers stopped to talk, and the ends of their cigarettes glowed red. Then they turned and retraced their steps.

When the soldiers were out of sight, Péter and the others pulled themselves up. They continued on along the row of trees. They were moving now with a greater sense of urgency than before. At the end of the field, where the soldiers had been standing, they came to a road. Beyond it was a forest. Once they were in among the trees again, they felt able to breathe a little more easily.

After tramping through the dark forest for a short time, the five men unexpectedly came upon a wide strip of cleared land.

'It's the border,' Péter said softly.

A few short steps away was the West, and freedom. But here the risk was also the greatest. Péter motioned to the others to be quiet. He listened out for any sounds that might indicate a patrol was nearby. Nothing disturbed the silence.

'Okay,' he said, 'Let's go.'

Together the five of them raced across the open space, and flung themselves into the trees on the far side.

Now the ground fell steeply away. Scrambling downwards, they soon came upon a narrow, unsheltered bench, carved roughly out of wood. It was just big enough to seat one person. Péter bent to examine the ground beneath the bench, his breath misting in the sharp air. Around him, the forest was utterly silent.

Suddenly, the harsh crackle of machine gun fire ripped through the night.

Péter whirled around. The noise had come from above and behind. It seemed to be back towards the cleared strip. It was a little further down from the point where they had crossed.

Alert, they listened, and waited. The burst of fire had been loud and prolonged. They could still hear the echo of it in their ears. But there was no more shooting. The silence returned. The men stared at each other.

Öcsi broke the quietness. 'Someone was not as lucky as us.'

Péter turned back to the wooden bench. He studied the ground around it. The snow was packed down from being trampled on, and there were traces of boot prints on the surface. The tension in Péter's face dissolved. He looked up at the others and smiled. An unassuming post, without the supporting paraphernalia of guard dogs and watchtowers. Signs of recent use. It could mean only one thing.

'It's where the Austrian border guard sits. There was someone here not long ago – before the last fall of snow.'

They were in Austria – they were safe.

Öcsi and Péter stood side by side. From their vantage point on the side of the hill, they could look out across the white valley ahead. The lights of houses winked below – an Austrian town. Already Péter felt suffused with calm. It was close to midnight on Boxing Day, and bitterly cold, but he didn't care. The worst was over; a different life awaited them.

Without looking back, he led his friends towards the lights.

Select Bibliography

Blackwood, Alan 1987 *The Hungarian Uprising*, USA: Rourke Enterprises

Gadney, Reg 1986 *Cry Hungary! Uprising 1956*, London: Weidenfeld & Nicolson

Hoffman, Eva 1993 *Exit into History: a Journey through the New Eastern Europe*, USA: Penguin Books

Jobbágyi, Gábor 1998 *Szigorúan Titkos Emlékkönyv*, Budapest: Szabad Tér Kiadó

Laping, Francis 1975 *Remember Hungary 1956*, USA: Alpha Publications, Inc.

Lomax, Bill (ed.) 1980 *Eyewitness in Hungary: The Soviet Invasion of 1956*, UK: Spokesman

Molnár, Miklós 2001 *A Concise History of Hungary*, UK: Cambridge University Press

Pongrátz, Gergely 1982 *Corvin Köz–1956*, Chicago: Self-published

Romsics, Ignác 1999 *Hungary in the Twentieth Century*, Budapest: Corvina Books Ltd.

Sugar, Peter *et al* (eds.) 1990 *A History of Hungary*, USA: Indiana University Press

Tőkés, Rudolf L. 1998 (reprinted) *Hungary's Negotiated Revolution: Economic reform, social change, and political sucession, 1957-1990*, UK: University Press, Cambridge

United Nations *Report of the Special Committee on the Problem of Hungary* General Assembly Official Records: eleventh session supplement no. 18 (A/3592), New York 1957

Acknowledgements

I am grateful most of all to the people who were prepared to share their experiences with me in such a frank and open way. This includes those whose stories are not presented here, in particular Péter Antal. Special thanks go to István Pálos and Tony Ámon, who were extremely generous with their time and resources, and helped me to believe that the project was worthwhile.

Many other people in both Australia and Hungary assisted me in various ways. I would like to thank Christine Balint and her parents for providing me with a way in to Melbourne's Hungarian community. Thanks to Duncan Shiels and Chris Mattheisen for information on current politics and culture in Hungary. Many thanks to Martin Zuba and Heather Elms for their contacts and friendship in Budapest. Thanks also to Éva Újfalusi for trying to teach me Hungarian.

Thanks also to Fran Bryson, Peter Bishop, Simon Gaythorpe, Dr Géza Kosa, Margaret Bearman, Hoa Pham and Liz Kemp, who all took the time to read earlier drafts. Your comments, suggestions and encouragement were invaluable.

I am indebted to the Eleanor Dark Foundation for granting me a fellowship at Varuna – The Writers' House, which enabled me to complete the manuscript. The support I received from residents and staff, especially Peter Bishop, was wonderful.

Finally, thanks to Mark Hempenstall for his patience and help with the process of publishing this edition.